"THE SCIENCE OF GREATNESS"

By:

Warren B.

&

James Jerome Bell

Contents

WISDOM, FROM ONE PLAYA' TO ANOTHER

As far back as "J" can remember, he has always been clever and industrious. When you grow up in a society that has a *conspiracy against black manhood*; it's best when you can learn to *think outside the box.* People who don't think in a conventional way are always in a better position to circumnavigate the obvious traps waiting for them. While everybody else is airing all their dirty laundry on Facebook, me and James are *thinking of a master plan.*

3

So often James and I feel exacerbated by all the rhetoric circulating back and forth between average-kick-a-rounds. It's almost as if no one has *a thought of their own* anymore. So much of what is on people's minds is stuff the media *chooses* for them. It would be nice if more people were cerebral enough to *read between the lines.*

But instead, people quote and regurgitate information like a bunch of stupid parrots. It's not that I want to tell people what to think. But rather, I just wish they weren't such sheeplike creatures.

Because of the *mechanical nature* of men, it has become easy for the power structure to influence them. You would think that more Americans would be *intelligent* enough to recognize when their government *lies* to them. But time after time, they fall for the same bullshit.

If the world bankers want a repeat of 1930, they could do it. Once the world bankers swindled President Nixon into taking America off the gold standard, they were in a better position to implement their agenda. "Give me *control of a nation's money*, and I care not who makes the laws," said Meyer Amsel Rothschild. Too often, people in Amerikkka make the mistake of assuming they are *in control* of their destinies. When the truth is, most people are nothing more than *machines*.

In 1929, machines thought they were *deciding* to pull their money out of the local bank. This hysteria was caused by a *lie* orchestrated by the powers that be, suggesting that local banks were *insolvent.* People, being the dumb robots they are, ran out to their local banks and *withdrew* all of their money. This action was caused by sheeplike fear, all manifested by *a little white lie.*

James and I are shepherds, *not sheep.* No one can *control* the way we think. If you aim to be a shepherd you will have to *take control of your thoughts, moods, and feelings.* In a world full of manipulation and trickery, the last thing you want to end up being is a *stupid animal* awaiting its slaughter.

Fortunately for us, James and I had loving families that created an atmosphere that allowed us to become our own people. Even with all the desperate attempts *principalities* have made to effeminize the black male, James and I have still emerged as *men.*

As *players,* we view a world as being an interesting mixture of positive and negative forces. And the truth is, we are not impressed with what we see in most people. There are few *real players* left in the world. What it takes for most guys to get noticed, James and I already have *in our back pockets.*

Often when we meet, we discuss the deformities inherent in most people's character. Instead of making full use of their God given rights to become *great,* people would much rather acquiesce to a life of *mediocrity.* It's sad to think that most people would forsake their ability to become *great* in exchange for *normality.* But it is what it is.

The main purpose of this book is to give its readers the key to *greatness*. Greatness cannot be achieved through the accumulation of money. Although River Phoenix had amassed more money than he could spend in a lifetime, Phoenix never achieved *greatness*. Greatness also cannot be achieved by becoming world famous. Elvis Presley was as well-connected as any person you could think of; but because Elvis lacked this *key*, he failed to become *great*.

Greatness can only be attained by understanding the scripture *John 10:14.* "Jesus answered them, Is it not written in your law, I said, *Ye are gods?*" People who lack this understanding will probably believe it is blasphemous to suggest that a man can become *a god.* At no time in Jesus's life did he say he was here to do the will of himself. What made

Jesus *a god* was he understood the key to greatness is *obedience (Luke 22:42)*.

Any man or woman can become *great*. The key is to learn how to submit your will to the will of the *Father*. Then, when you speak, it will be the *Father* speaking through you. When you achieve, it will be the *Father* achieving through you. Man will always come up short in his own understanding. But if he will only learn how to *listen* to the *still small voice* of God within him, he will undoubtedly become *great*.

In speaking of those who lack *greatness*, nothing could be more trifling than believing God certain people a *moral* right to *own* someone else. Working to pay off a prior debt or serving as a *worker-slave* due to becoming a *prisoner of war* is not the same thing as being *dehumanized* by someone.

The privileges that white people enjoy in this country are a direct result of *white supremacy,* not *greatness.* Just because certain whites do not *aggressively participate* in white supremacy, does not change the benefits they *inactively receive* as a result of it.

For years, *whites* have fought tooth and nail against those who *tell the truth.* It takes a *strong man* to tell the truth when he knows he's standing in a belly full of lies.

Not even Jesus was exempt from being hated for *telling the truth.* Jesus wasn't no punk. He *aggressively* turned over the money tables in the church and openly condemned the *Pharisees* of his time. That doesn't sound like an *innocent little lamb* to you, does it?

For this reason, the Roman government charged Jesus with sedition. Sedition means, "Agitation against the authority of a state." Jesus wasn't some *docile white sheep* who knew his *place* and stayed in it.

As in Jesus's day, the goal of the *few in power* is to make sure that all bearers of truth *look evil* in the eyes of the masses. That way, when the government tries to do away with them, society's *puppets* will inadvertently make themselves available for the job. Slaves!

Although many rappers claim to be *players* and *pimps,* me and "J" were *born* into the game. We weren't *recruited.* People often say that *genes* play a huge role in determining what a person becomes in life. This is only partly true. The other major factor is *environmental*. With that said, there is another influence that is rarely discussed by most people. That is the influence caused by the *will* of man.

Genetic and environmental influences fall under the banner of *fate*. Fate is the sum total of all of a person's influences and experiences. People who do not use their *willpower* to overcome the *magnetic pull* of fate will join the ranks of men who are governed by *outside influences*.

But there are *a* few of us who *refuse* to lie down to the power of fate. Such people have a supernatural quality, which helps them to manifest their *destiny*. *Destiny* cannot be reached by merely hoping or praying for it. It can only come as a result of *a few simple disciplines practiced everyday.*

Michael Dell, of Dell computers once said: "Swing for *hits,* not for home runs." When you learn how to *stack* the positive results of *small achievements* on top of each other, you will be well on your way to becoming a major success in life.

People often think they have to take huge *steps* to achieve big things. But most big accomplishments are a result of many *smaller steps or achievements.* When every player is proficient at *swinging for hits;* the bases will be *loaded* when the fourth batter comes up to the plate. And if that fourth batter just so happens to *hit a home run,* this will represent four well-earned runs for the team.

This is how the *game of life* should be played. If you intend to have success in life, you must *stack the deck* in your favor. Success is no accident. It is the result of doing certain things everyday in a certain way.

On the flip side of success is *failure.* Failure can be defined as: "A few simple *errors in judgment* practiced everyday." The same *process* that leads you to success can also lead you to a failure. Failure is a result of putting off small tasks that you *could* or *should* be doing.

Even something as *small* as not putting a stamp on an important document and mailing it could be the beginning of a negative snowball effect. Why, because everything that you do *or don't do* in life affects everything else.

Remember, success is the result of *a few simple disciplines practiced everyday.* By neglecting to do the *simple tasks* that lead to success, you will have *no excuses* when you finally fail. Understanding this *little lesson* alone is worth more than the price of this book!

Another point about success is that success begins with *doing what you love to do.* No matter what your place is in life, I believe everyone has *something* to offer. Even a janitor whose work brings him a deep sense of *pleasure* is *successful.* There are plenty of people who are not rich but who are successful. And there are plenty of people who have money but who are unsuccessful.

The key is to find a *niche* and then become proficient at it. Although being rich does not automatically make you successful, it will still be easier to become rich once you take what you do naturally to the highest level. *Riches come as a result of providing the world with a great service.* The more proficient you are at providing a unique service, the more money you will attract.

And soon, *the whole world* may become interested in having *you* provide your unique service to them. At this point, there's no limit to how rich you can become. But remember, becoming rich is always the result of *finding a need and filling it.* You may not have ever dreamed of becoming rich. But if you will only consider the words mentioned above, you may well be on your way to becoming rich and successful.

Solomon once said, "A wise man leaves an inheritance for his children and his children's children." I quoted this scripture because it is in your best interest to be rich and successful. Why settle for *just enough* to live on when you can have *more than enough*? It is only *wise* that a man consider how much in *cash* and *assets* he would like to have before he dies. And it is also wise that he *plan* on having *more than enough* to take care of his children and his grandchildren.

If the trend in most communities is to leave one's posterity with *little,* I say it's time you *break* that trend. Plan on being rich or at least well to do by the time you die. Never entertain thoughts of poverty or struggle.

If your parents were poor and wanting when you were growing up, never allow your thoughts to *focus* on those times. Leave your past behind you. Only entertain thoughts of prosperity. *You cannot attract wealth by thinking about poverty.* Think only about success!

Next, you must determine what success *looks like* for you. Create a mental *image of success* and keep your mind focused on that *picture*. This is what is meant by the biblical phrase *pray without ceasing.* In other words, keep your mental picture on the forefront of your thoughts *without ceasing* <u>until</u> it comes to fruition. Master this principle and you will turn your *fate* into your *destiny.*

Being that James and I have a certain *Je ne sais quoi,* we are more inclined to *read between the lines.* While most people believe *whatever* their government places in front of them, we can always tell when something smells *fishy.* We are not prone to influences that come from *outside* of our intelligence.

This intelligence also affords us the ability to *read* people. Unlike many whites in Amerikkka, our ability to *read people* is not the same concept as *prejudging* them. James and I have a distinct ability to *see through people.* This ability is often misunderstood by those closest to us. While we may understand the intricacies of this gift, most people assume we are prejudging people we do not know.

This is also the reason "J" and I have so much trouble trying to work for others. Because we can *see through* people, managers often feel *intimidated* by their inability to *create fear* in us. People can *feel* when they are having the right *affect* on others.

Most *managers* in any business are insecure. They often feel they have to *pull rank* or prove they have the *authority.* Whenever such people come across an employee who does not *fear them,* managers will work hard to prove that they are, *in charge.*

On the flip side of this fact is that, the higher up you go in corporate America, the *nicer* people tend to be. The *owners* of a big business don't have to *prove* anything to anybody. Everyone knows their *position.* When you're already *at the top,* you don't have to doggedly *claw your way* up. If more people only knew how to balance their insecurities in the workplace, work could be a more pleasant environment.

For that reason, James and I are comrades. We understand the dynamics of *animal fear* and human psychology. This gives us a decided *edge* in the world.

Since most people don't understand society, they don't have the privilege of *avoiding* it. While most people would give their left arm to rub shoulders with *the beautiful people* of the world, James and I often find ourselves *bored to death* with them. "Knowledge is pain!"

When I'm *impressed* with someone I try to *make contact* with them. But when I'm not, I *turn my back* on them. It's important that you *choose* friends who share the same level of *understanding* as you. When you find that your closest constituents lack the same ambition, the time may have come for you to *move on.*

You can't be afraid of *change.* "Change is necessary for growth." Whenever the universe has made the *nest* too uncomfortable, it means it is time for you to *fly away.* Never mind what the people closest to you think.

Sometimes, it is best to *keep silent* about your plans until they have been accomplished. The last thing you want is for the people you love to *shoot bullets* at your dreams. Keep all *busters* at bay until the time is right.

This brings "J" and I to another important point. It is always best you remain *true* to yourself! Never force yourself to hang with people you are *superior* to. And by superior, I mean in *thought.* If the people you hang out with don't *want more* than they currently have, they are *dying a slow death.* You deserve *more* than that!

Most people are *content* with where they are. It is only natural that we desire to have *more* than we currently have. But too often, people become complacent and lose their zeal for *new experiences.* Remember, *God wants you to have more because the more you have, the more He can do through you.*

And then there is the importance of being well traveled. Many say that travel broadens your perspective. It is important you venture to new cities, states, and countries to make yourself more *familiar* with their culture and way of life. Far too many people are only familiar with the borough from which they grew up.

People like this may never take advantage of all the *world* has to offer.

For many, the only time they get to do any traveling is when someone either dies or is getting married. But extensive travel should be high on your priority list. If you haven't already done this, you should make a list of all the places you want to see before you die. Then, get your finances in order and *do it.*

Young men should travel because it will make them *worldlier.* This will only *add* to their maturity and understanding. If the people in your circumference are too *stiff* to venture out beyond the familiar, ditch them and get yourself some *new friends.* The last thing you want is to have a life of regrets.

Another point we'd like to discuss is the subject of *individuality*. There is nothing wrong with being a basic *ordinary guy*. As we will state in this book, not everyone can be charismatic. But, you do not want to just be *average*. Average people are like an old decrepit building. You know that it's there when you drive by it, but you never pay it any attention.

You don't want to be so nondistinguishable that you become just *another face in the crowd*. If you were a *hand* in a card game, what *cards* or characteristics are your strongest? *Identify* those cards and then *use them* to your advantage. The key to this technique is found in the *science of thought*.

Whatever a man thinks about grows. Whenever you are in the company of others, simply *focus your attention* on your strengths. *Thoughts are seeds.* Whenever you *focus your attention* on something, the *seeds* of your thoughts get *planted* into the minds of others.

Whenever you are in a crowd of people, *focus your attention* on your strengths. Never mind if other people in the room seem to have more strengths than you. *Just keep your mind focused on the truth.* Suddenly, you will find yourself having a conversation with a interesting person.

A thought held in the mind of a man affects the thoughts of the people around him. So, it makes no sense to focus your attention on your weaknesses. They don't exist! *The only thing that matters is the truth. The positive is the truth, the whole truth, and nothing but the truth.* Keep practicing this technique until it becomes a *habit.* Then, when you make your first *million,* you can send me my *10 percent.*

Another point we wish to lament is the importance of *money.* In our lifetimes, "J" and I have known all types. We have known squares that were always broke and we have also known squares that always had money. We have known great players who were poor, but who owned several nice *things.* We have also known players who were *balling* at the top of their games.

The key difference between these individuals is their *philosophy. A man's philosophy in life is who he is.* "You are what you think about." Many street hustlers and players chump off their money in exchange for extravagance. For them, getting their *shine on* is more important than *building wealth* as a result of asset acquisition.

For many players, their *philosophies* rest largely on expressing *ghetto fabulousness.* Ghetto fabulous is a term I use to describe a lifestyle of *bold and flashy poverty.* It is a lifestyle based on the *accumulation* of *shiny things.* The main reason I define ghetto fabulousness as *bold and flashy poverty* is because of its inability to provide its owners with *residual income.* Ultimately, the *shiny things* ghetto fabulous people *invest* their money in cannot be resold for a *profit.*

In the end, this lifestyle leads to *poverty* because it fails to produce consistent streams of income. Having a consistent stream of income that more than supports your lifestyle is called *wealth*.

True wealth is not measured in the accumulation of material goods. It is measured in *time*. In other words, if you stopped working today, *how far ahead would you be of your monthly expenses*? Most people are not even *two months ahead.* So they *have to work* or keep hustling to take care of their monthly obligations. There is another term often used to describe this. It's called *the rat race!*

Rather than us go into "The Science of Money," we urge you to first determine what a *life of security* would mean to you. For instance, could you *live well* on a monthly budget of $5,000 a month? If so, what *lifestyle* could this budget afford you? Answering this question will help you to better *visualize* the lifestyle you want to live.

Once you can determine what lifestyle you want to have, you must then determine *how much monthly income* you would need to sustain that lifestyle. Doing this mental exercise will help you to bring your *dreams* into the realm of *reality.* Knowing how the *numbers add up* will show you how feasible your dreams are.

Next, set a financial goal to become *wealthy.* Once you know what you want out of life, your next goal is to become *financially secure.* Being six months ahead financially is a great way to start. For instance, if your goal for *security* can be achieved with a monthly income of *$5,000 a month,* you should begin by saving at least *$30,000 dollars*. By doing this you will

not be *rich*, but you will be *wealthy*.

And here I must reiterate the importance

of thinking long and hard about the *lifestyle* you

want. The reason this is important is because

life is not about getting what you want. It's about

wanting it after you get it. Knowing for sure

what you want will save you the trouble of

working hard to acquire something that won't

bring you any fulfillment.

Like "J" and I already said, success has

more to do with *happiness* than it does with

acquiring money or fame. True happiness can

only come from *within*. But it is hard not to be

happier when you know you are *wealthy*.

The second benefit of building wealth is the *comfort* it gives you. Life is less stressful when you had the wisdom to secure a *nest egg* for you and your family. Life happens fast. Why not be prepared for it?

Follow these simple guidelines and you will be well on your way to creating a full and complete life.

THE *SCIENCE* OF GREATNESS!

"J" and I recently read an article entitled: *What makes a man?* It was written by a black woman who was postulating her *understanding* of what qualities represent true manhood. Today, it is painfully obvious that most black men do not *understand* what it means to be a *man.* And to be honest, I doubt many black women understand this subject either.

Among the first points we would like to make about manhood is that real men are *focused.* Solomon once said: "For, without a *vision*, the people perish." A man does not have to know exactly *how* he will reach his goal. But he at least has to have a *specific* goal to reach.

This is important because what you attract in life is based on your *thoughts*. For instance, if a man's life is governed by a *philosophy of survival*, he is not going to be successful. Survival is good for *animals*. But *man* is supposed to use his mind to *create* what he wants.

The *intellectual center* in man is what is supposed to separate him from the animals. But if man does not make full use of this capacity, he will live a menial existence. On the heavenly plane, *light* did not exist before the Creator *imagined it* in His Mind. Thus, we see that *imagination is the first seed of manifestation.*

The problem with man is that he does not realize that he too can *create* on the same lines as the Father. Man must use his *imagination* to perceive a *better reality* for himself. And only after he envisions a better reality does he need a *helpmate* to *help him* achieve it.

I would also like to add that a man cannot even *attract* a suitable helpmate without first having a worthy *ideal* to achieve. The universe is more than *ready* to supply you with everything you need. But it cannot help you achieve something that *doesn't exist* in your imagination.

More important than having *a means to an end* is having an *idea* of what that *end* will be. The support staff, the financial backing, the spiritual favor, and everything else you *need* will

come once you *know* exactly what you want.
Once you *know* what you want, you should
never be afraid to ask the Father to give it to
you. "Do not be like them, for your father knows
what you *need* before you ask him" (Matthew
6:8).

There are many success stories about
ordinary people doing extraordinary things. But
the secret to their success is rarely emphasized.
The secret to all achievement is *attraction.* For
many people, they believe *hard work* is the key
to achievement. And while I agree with this
premise, I don't know if many people understand
why.

The hard work of achievement is *proper
thought.* Maintaining your focus on a specific
goal is the hardest work you will ever do.

Without a singular focus, no one can achieve lasting success.

If you wanted to send a friend an important text, you wouldn't send them all the letters of the alphabet in their proper order and trust they will be able to make out your message. You would send them a *specific* message! This same principle applies to man's ability to create whatever he wants.

Any goal you set for yourself must be *specific.* People with vague and nebulous dreams will never achieve *greatness.* You cannot properly *lead* a family or business if you don't know *where* you are going? But what must also accompany the setting of a specific goal is the *process* of achieving it.

For instance, if you want to successfully plant tulip seeds you must first *till the soil,* then you must *plant the seeds,* then you have to *protect the seeds,* and then water the seeds, and finally, you have to *wait.* This same process is necessary to manifest whatever you conjure in your imagination.

The *tilling* aspect of creating what you want lies in *breaking up your old habits.* The number one habit you will need to *break* is allowing your mind to wander aimlessly from one thought to another. No matter what anyone says, the mind of man can only focus on *one thing* at a time. You will never be successful in life without learning how to *focus* your mind on a definite aim.

The *planting* aspect of creating what you want lies in imputing your mental picture into your subconscious mind. Once you are successful at convincing your subconscious that what you want is *real,* you then have to *protect your seed* from the *birds* of life.

For many people on the path of achievement, *family can often be your worst enemy.* The Temptations once sang a song called: "I'm Losing You." It's a story about a man who can tell that he is *losing his grip* on his woman. It begins with the words: "I know you want to leave me, but I refuse to let you go."

In truth, this is a song of *desperation.* It shows the peculiar position some people find themselves in when the person they love is about to *leave them.* In the same way, the people closest to you could be your greatest *obstacle* to success. People can *feel* when there's something *different* about you.

Once you set out to achieve something *greater* than the people around you, they often start using certain mental tactics to *pull you back down to their reality.* In other words, *they know they are losing you.* This part of the process of success is called *protecting the seeds.* People who work against your desires for advancement represent the *birds* of life. They are called *birds* because their main purpose is to *pluck away the seeds* of your dreams.

In certain cases, the *birds* of life could be your wife, husband or lover. No matter how much you love your significant other, *if they are holding you back, you probably don't have a chance.* So pay close attention to the people around you. You may just have to *plant your seeds* at night while all the *birds* are asleep. In other words, keep your goals a *secret* until you manifest them. If the people around you do not have a working plan in action you should keep your plans to yourself.

The next aspect in the *process* of success is the *watering* effect. Watering the seeds of your goals means keeping your attention *focused* on them. As I said before, the mind of man can only focus on *one thing* at a time. That is why it is preposterous to try to be successful at accomplishing *ten different tasks* at once. Achievement requires a *singular focus on a definite aim.* By focusing your attention on a specific goal *without ceasing,* you will be *watering* the seeds of your vision. Although this task may seem easy, it will be the hardest task you will ever commit to.

The final aspect in the *process* of success is the *waiting effect.* By *waiting* I do not mean sitting back and twiddling your thumbs. Waiting means *thanksgiving* and *expectation.* You cannot expect to receive what you ask of the Father without having a certain measure of *faith. Faith means living your life as though you already posses the goal you desire.*

God does not want his children to be *poor!* The reason is because the more wealth you have, the more the Father can accomplish *through* you. *Being poor will not allow you to express God's love to the fullest extent.* If your heart is in the right place, you should ask for much *more* than you now have. Then, *water* that desire by *thanking the Father in advance* for what He is *giving* you. Follow these few steps and you will achieve whatever your heart desires.

Any man who has a *personal relationship* with the Father should be at the *top* of every woman's priority list. Why would any *sensible* woman reject a man who has achieved *greatness*? Anything other than this is *settling*.

The main purpose of this book is to give its readers the key to *greatness*. Greatness cannot be achieved through the accumulation of money. Although J.P. Morgan had amassed more money than he could spend in a lifetime, Morgan never achieved *greatness*. Greatness also cannot be achieved by becoming world famous. Anna Nicole Smith was as well connected as any person you could think of; but because Anna lacked this *key,* she failed to become *great.*

Greatness can only be attained by understanding the scripture *John 10:14.* "Jesus answered them, Is it not written in your law, I said, *Ye are gods?*" People who lack this understanding will probably believe it is blasphemous to suggest that a man can become *a god.* At no time in Jesus' life did he say he was here to do the will of himself. What made Jesus *a god* was that he understood the key to greatness is *obedience (Luke 22:42).*

Any man or woman can become *great.* The key is to learn how to submit your will to the will of the *Father.* Then, when you speak, it will be the *Father* speaking *through* you. When you achieve, it will be the *Father* achieving

through you. Man will always come up short in

his own understanding. But if he will only learn

how to *listen* to the *still small voice* of God within

him, he will undoubtedly become *great*.

In addition to *greatness*, any man wishing

to improve his standard of living must make a

point of only hanging out with *like-minded*

people. In life you will either be *guilty* by

association or *blessed* by it. Good or bad

association is a *choice* we all have to make.

Success always comes with a *price*. And

dropping your loser friends and family may be

the *price* you will have to pay to be successful. I

say these words not to be mean or insensitive.

But rather so you won't have any *excuses* to stay

in your present condition if that is not what you want.

Men must have a *resolve* to be rich and successful no matter what. In other chapters, I dealt with the importance of men letting women *choose* them. In this chapter I will deal more with *becoming* the man you want to be.

So often, I see men acquiesce to the wishes of women. I know I will not be popular for saying this, but many women don't even know what they want. As a man you've got to *know* what you want out of life. At the same time, you've got to accept that not every woman wants what you want.

There may be some women you might want to get with. But that doesn't mean *they are for you.* Every man must have a *program*!

And if a woman wants to get with *you* she will have to get with *your program.* Although this may sound vain and egotistical, I assure you it is not.

In every business or organization there is a *manager* or *boss.* That manager or boss is there for one main reason; to *lead* the team to success. In the book of "Esther," you may recall the only reason Esther got a shot at becoming *queen* was because *Vashti* was trying to be *independent.*

Queen Vashti must have fell and bumped her head and forgot that King Ahasuerus was *in charge.* Although the world will say *times have changed,* certain things just represent *order. God is not the author of confusion!* He is a God of *order.*

Malcolm X once said: "In every organization, *someone must be the boss.*" "Even if it's just one person; you've got to be the boss of yourself." There must always be a chain of command. There must be a *leader.*

Except for those men with *momma issues* or who are *mommas' boys,* it is only *natural* that a man be the *leader.* Why, because *energy* says so. As a man my energy is *yang. Yang is a masculine* and *giving energy.* A woman's energy is *yen.* And yen energy is *feminine* and *receiving.* It is through the universal principle of "gender" that God created everything in existence.

Men must never get into a *power struggle* with females. If the female you are dealing with is a *lady* she will automatically understand your position. If she is a *woman* it can go either way.

But if she a *bitch*, she will *never* understand. As

you can see there is a difference between a *lady*,

a *woman*, and a *bitch*.

Ladies are always *feminine* and *classy* in

every way. They are *seen* and rarely heard. But

when they do speak, everybody listens. *Women*

on the other hand often teeter back and forth

between *femininity* and *masculinity*. Ultimately,

this is an *identity crisis* issue.

If such a *challenge* takes place *early* in the

relationship, it can be forgiven. But if it proves

to be *ongoing*, it might be time for you to *drop*

the package and start over again – clean.

Truthfully, a *bitch* shouldn't even have

your number unless she's just a *booty call*.

Bitches are what males get when they *bottom*

feed. Most *bitches* are loud and severely lacking in *class.* If your girl is on the phone and everyone in the room keeps looking at her while she's talking, she's probably a *bitch.*

Bitches never try to elevate their level of *understanding.* For instance, if you were to tell a bitch that she *talks too loudly in public,* she'll probably reply: "Oh well, my voice just carries!" *Bitches* aren't interested in changing themselves. For them, *it is what it is.*

A *lady* is always the highest female on the *ladder of femininity.* A woman is almost always under a *lady* but is always higher than the *bitch.* If you are a *man* and you require some *peace of mind* in your home, I strongly suggest you only date *ladies.* That is, unless you come across a *woman* with an *open mind.*

As a rule, I never date women who either already know everything or don't want to learn anything new. If a female is unwilling to learn, I drop her ass *quickly* and throw up the *deuces* on that ass. Black men, if you have any *balls* left in this racist ass society, I suggest you do the same.

One of the key characteristics all *ladies* respect in a *man* is *self-control.* There are many guys out here who are more *emotional* than their women. Not even *women* respect a man who is too emotional. *All females* want to *know that when a challenging situation occurs, her man is going to step up to the plate and take charge.*

Men who have no control over their *thoughts, moods, and feelings* are not fit to be called *men.* Men are always *firm* but do at times show their women that they have *emotion*. This is necessary for *balance*.

What's often never admitted by most black *women* is that most of them would rather date a *boy* than a *real man*. I can tell what most black women *want* because *I see* what most black women *choose*. I tell sisters all the time *you cannot separate who you are with, from who you are*. A woman's man is an *exact reflection* of herself.

In truth, the best way to look at your significant other is as a *mirror*. Your lover is *the truth, the whole truth, and nothing but the truth* about *where you are* in your personal development. Instead of establishing *higher standards* for themselves, women should focus more on developing a *higher level of being.* Why, because you are what you attract!

On that same token, black men need *higher standards* than a phat ass and a pretty face. An *intelligent* rich man may still choose a *bitch* to be his lawfully wedded wife. Ask Tiger Woods. The *bitch* was a fucking *nanny* for Christ sakes! A *real woman* like Hillary Clinton would have been in Tiger's corner no matter what transpired. You feel me?

That's why I say that black men need to set *higher standards* for themselves. What is your woman bringing to the table? Does she have her own money? Is she *classy* enough to represent you *the right way* when you are not around? Or, is she *loud, rude,* and *always in need of money* to get her hair and nails *did*?

I know it may be hard for some of you, but men need females who can *help them* to become successful. Period! If you have a *working plan* and your woman is unwilling to support you, drop her ass.

Rarely does anyone talk about the *standards* that *black men* should have. We only seem to discuss a *black woman's* standards. Timeout for that! Men, it's time you set some higher standards for yourself. And while you're at it, I suggest you leave them *snow rats* alone.

Look if I'm going to deal with some bullshit, it might as well be with a *black* woman. Look at "Narjes Golabbakhsh" who *randomly blamed a "black man with a tattoo" for kidnapping and killing her baby.* Lying ass! I hate to say it but it is so easy for certain *white women* to make false allegations against *brothers*.

Look at that whole "Rosewood massacre" that took place in rural Levy County, Florida. This whole incident was spawned by a *devil* named: Frances "Fannie" Taylor, who claimed she was *assaulted by a black man.*

Because of this *little white lie*, "Sam Carter," a local blacksmith and teamster who worked for Turpentine Still was killed. He was tortured, fatally shot in the face, and then had his mutilated body hanged from a tree. The purpose of this demonic activity was to be a *symbol* to other black men in the area *not to fuck with white women.* Later, the entire town of Rosewood was destroyed by vigilantes.

And let's not forget about the *race riot of
Tulsa, Oklahoma (Black Wall Street) on the
morning of May 30, 1921.* The whole *massacre*
was spawned by an incident in which Dick
Rowland grabbed a white woman's arm to *brace
his fall* as he tripped into an elevator. This
incident caused the white elevator operator
Sarah Page to *flee the elevator in a panic.*
Accounts of the incident circulated in the white
community during the day and naturally became
more *exaggerated* as the day went on.

In the early morning hours of June 1,
1921, "Black Wall Street" was looted and burned
to the ground by white rioters and *government*
airplanes. Over 800 people were treated for
injuries and the estimated reports of deaths
stood at upwards of 300 people.

Anyone can fall in love with someone of a different race. *But history speaks louder than emotion!* When Malcolm X was sentenced to 10 years for armed robbery, no one even asked him about the *validity* of the charges. *All those whites could think about was whether he was having sex with Sophia!*

Wisdom tells us that *if you don't learn from history, it will repeat itself!* If you are black and you have *forgotten the screams and burning flesh of your ancestors,* you *deserve* whatever you got coming. Just ask Tiger Woods. Again, if I am going to deal with some bullshit, it might as well be with a black woman.

Now, we too have our issues. But they are *our issues!* I have often felt frustrated in my dealings with black women. But I *love* them!

And one of the attributes of love is *patience.* If I expect black women to deal with *my* issues, I will also have to deal with theirs. One such issue is self-confidence.

Although self-confidence is important, there are some sisters out there who feel *threatened* by a man with an *abundance* of it. And by *abundance* I do not mean *arrogance.* I mean genuine self-confidence.

For instance, a black woman who was very interested in me once told me that I have "A God complex." What she was trying to convey was that she felt I see myself in *too high* of a light. What she did not understand was that I am only living *John 10:14.* At every man's highest level of spiritual development, he is *a god!* Although no man is "THE ALL, IN ALL;" every man does have the *potential* to become more *like* "THE ALL."

Confidence can be contagious. But sometimes it can be a *threat* to people who don't understand it. Any woman who is not equally as confident in herself should not *choose* a man with a huge ego. Remember, it takes a *Michelle* to snag a Barack. Anything *less* will not do.

A real man must be able to challenge a woman's understanding and even *teach her things* she may not know. But he will never do this in a *patriarchal spirit.* Mature men are never overbearing. They only teach a woman what she is *ready* to learn.

Another attribute of real men is that they have learned how to *listen* to women. Some men who are very strong-willed often have a tendency to be macho. *But the wisest of all men are those who have learned to listen to their wives.*

If you are with the *right* woman, she has *something* you don't have. What's the sense of having something powerful at your disposal if you don't make *use* of it? I once knew a powerful black woman who was working as an assistant for an alleged *man of God.*

Although he was the *Pastor* of the church, I could tell he did not have the leadership skills to take his church to the next level. But his *assistant* did. Even though he had many *spiritual* gifts, he failed to *see* what God was trying to do. Had he understood the definition of *greatness* as outlined in this book, he would have known *why* his assistant was in his life.

But instead, he failed to *see* it. And now, that *window of opportunity* has closed on him.

Although Jesus had many disciples, *Mary Magdalene* was the most *dedicated* disciple of them all. All men boast of their strength and unmovable resolve in the *thick* of things. But how many will claim they know you in the *thin?* When Jesus was going through his trial, *all of the men ran away,* except John. *But the females stood by the master!*

There's no question that to this day, the *female* is still the *principle disciple* in the church. Preachers, who are too *egotistical* to make full use of all the *treasures* at their disposal, will suffer the consequences of *limitation.* There is no excuse for those who do not understand the "Law of Use."

The "Law of Use" says, "If you do not *use* what you have, someone else has the right to *take* it!" And that goes for *all of us* who do not make full use of what we have been given.

Among the number one *commodities* many of us misuse is *time*. Malcolm X once said: "In all of our deeds, the proper *value* and *respect* for time determines success or failure." Malcolm was time conscious to a tee. In fact, he once lamented: "I don't drive by my speedometer, I drive by my watch."

We've all got to examine how we spend our *time*. My earnest prayer is that the *Spirit of God* would *guide me* more and more everyday to make the right moves at the *right time*. That way, I too can enjoy the full benefits that come with being *great*.

BE – A – MAN!

For every *male* there is one *female*. But for every *man* there's at least *100 women*. Once a male reaches the coveted level of *manhood,* his range of possibilities broadens.

Overall, *real women* are attracted to *real men.* So often in the black community, black women face the frustrations of dealing with grown ass *boys masquerading as men.* Since women mature faster than men, *real women* are inclined to seek a relationship with a mature intelligent man.

On the flip side, is the often misunderstood relationship between a black woman's *desire* to have a real man and her innate *fear* of one. Most black women have been *abused* by no good black *males.* It is always easier for a *victim* to expect the worst from men who remind her of her earlier *predators.* This plays itself out when an *abused black woman* finally links herself with a *real black man.*

For most people, *falling in love* is a scary situation. Love is the most exhilarating and fearful experience anyone could ever have. There is no greater level of *vulnerability* one can experience than when *in love.* You are never more *open* to hurt and disappointment than when your *heart* is exposed. Too often the *predators* who helped raise black women *abused* them when they should have been *protecting* them. So, I understand the fear.

Why should black women extend their trust to a black man when their own fathers, stepfathers, brothers, uncles, and momma's boyfriends took advantage of them in every way imaginable? This is the untold story that so often goes on in the black community. But we must not forget that not all black men are predators!

The flip side of this, of course is Amerikkka's malevolent plot to reduce the black man's *importance* to the size of a pigmy. Take away a man's ability to provide for himself and his family and you enable the fracturing of his self-esteem. With few opportunities left in Amerikkka for black men to take advantage of, all that seems left for many of them to *conquer* is the *weakest members* among them.

For many of us, the only females who seem to be *happy to see us* come around are our *daughters, stepdaughters, nieces,* and *younger female friends of the family.* Most other black women have already been *programmed* to see us in a negative light. These realities often create many issues within the family unit.

I do not condone any form of sexual, psychological or emotional abuse stemming from such dire conditions. But, I would not be *human* if I did not *try to understand* how these treacherous environmental influences can produce such sad effects.

Because of the *dysfunction* festering in the black community, it's no wonder why true

"Black Love" is so hard to find. These *dysfunctions* are also why it is so easy for sisters to become *sexual objects* for men.

For many black girls, the only way they can experience *closeness* with a man is when they are having sex. There are many young black females today who sleep around with guys, but who are not *promiscuous*. These girls are only seeking that *feeling of closeness* they lacked as a child. This *giving up of their bodies* is made easier to do since their father's, brother's or even close friends of the family have already *taken their innocence* early on.

Black men and women must be *mindful* of how their experiences are affecting their current relationships. Black men must become more aware of how a black woman's *insecurities* and *fears* are inhibiting her from *trusting* or *submitting* to him. Black men and women must also have a large reservoir of *patience* as they seek to help their partners *get pass their past.*

Black women must also be aware of how their *fears* and *insecurities* cause them to *take black men through the ringer* rather than allowing *us* to *love them.* Black women must also be careful not to let their *fears of intimacy* cause them to *sabotage* a good thing. This is important. It is always easier to kill something that has the potential to grow and later hurt you, than to let it mature and become something powerful. But you cannot achieve this goal without *introspection.*

The essence of manhood requires men to become self-aware. The beginning of all understanding begins with *inner standing*. No one can understand someone else without first understanding himself. Once a man understands his *thoughts, moods, and feelings;* he will possess the power to deal with the opposite sex. And once he understands himself, he can begin to understand the world at large.

No man can give something he does not already have. And once a man reaches a higher level of *being,* he will invariably become more *valuable.* Such a *value* will not only be respected by his woman, but it will also be respected by society. That is why I began this chapter by saying that for every *male* there is *one* woman, but for every *real man* there is at least *100 women.*

When I speak of *100 women,* it is only to show that *every black woman needs a real man.* And that goes for immature sisters who often waste their youth looking for love in all the wrong places. As we can see, *real black men* desperately need to answer the call to duty. A duty not to go and fight overseas in a war that will only benefit the rich. But the call of duty to his own race.

Black men must also stop *following* the white man in his pervertedness and homosexuality. There is nothing that can maneuver the essence of manhood in the wrong direction more than this. Such acts have always been a part of the European's culture. But they are not meant for the true and original "Suns of God."

Black women who are self-aware must also make a greater effort to instill confidence and pride in the black man. They must know that a black man is not *weak* just because he looks to his *support system (the black woman)*. The only reason a black man looks for support from his black woman is because that's part of the reason God created her.

Black men who are conscious must also do everything in their power to steer clear of the white man's courts and jails. These are not places for a *king* to waste his time. Amerikkkan society is largely governed by a race of men who lack spirituality and *leadership*. No spiritual *leader* would create a *cage* to house a human being. *Jails* do not reflect the black man's lack of humanity any more than the *slave chains* that once adorned his neck. In fact, the entire penal system is *proof* the white man is not a "Sun of God."

A "Sun of God" never seeks to be in *authority* over others. He does not seek to be *superior* to anyone. He is also not governed by a *competitive* spirit. And he is never concerned with what *devils* think about him.

The purpose of this book is to give the "Suns of God" the key to *greatness*. Greatness cannot be achieved through the accumulation of money. Although Sid Vicious was a high-profile individual, he never achieved *greatness*. Greatness also cannot be achieved by becoming world famous. Kurt Cobain was as well connected as any person you could think of; but because Kurt lacked this *key*, he failed to become *great*.

Greatness can only be attained by understanding the scripture *John 10:14.* "Jesus answered them, Is it not written in your law, I said, *Ye are gods?"* People who lack this understanding will probably believe it is blasphemous to suggest that a man can become *a god.* At no time in Jesus's life did he say he was here to do the will of himself. What made Jesus *a god* was that he understood the key to greatness is *obedience (Luke 22:42).*

Any man or woman can become *great.* The key is to learn how to submit your will to the will of the *Father.* Then, when you speak, it will be the *Father* speaking through you. When you achieve, it will be the *Father* achieving through you. Man will always come up short in his own understanding. But if he will only learn

how to *listen* to the *still small voice* of God within him, he will become *great.*

In this country, many white people feel the only people who deserve to be called *human* are the people *they decide* to treat as such. *White people's humanity rests solely on the way they treat others.* And to be honest, most whites have failed the *human test.*

Malcolm X once said, "If somebody is *winning* all the time it's not because they are *winning.*" "It's because they're *cheating.*" Real men do not have to cheat to get ahead. All they have to do is learn how to *listen* to the voice of God within. To become more acquainted with this *voice,* man must take the time to *sit quietly and listen to it.* This task will probably be the most difficult and wise thing man will ever do.

You can either practice *listening* early in the morning when everyone else is asleep or do it late at night. True *manhood* requires us to get *in-tune* to our higher self. How else can we know *when* and *what* we *should* do in certain instances? The worst thing any of us can do is allow our *egos* to play God. Those who make this mistake always find themselves in a worse predicament. So be wise and *listen.*

And remember, *women choose, men pursue...* Over the years, I have seen what can happen when a man tries to *force his Mack hand* on a woman. If she did not *choose him* these situations almost always end badly. The reason is overanxious men tend to disregard the *laws of mating.* Such laws require men to relax and let the women do the choosing.

Men must also have the confidence to be seen and not heard. If there's one fact I know about women it's that they're always watching. Men who don't understand this tend to be too aggressive or loud with or around women. Unless you are trying to scare her off, it is better that you learn to curb your enthusiasm and take it easy.

The most powerful men on earth have learned how to govern their responses with *measured emotions.* The reason this is important is because all men have two heads. One head is resting on the top of his shoulders. And the second head is resting between his legs. No matter how fine a woman is, men must have the strength to *control* their animal passions. Like men, women are also part *animal.* They too possess the same sexual desires as men. The only difference is, most women are better at *controlling* or *disguising* their lusts. This control factor gives women a decided *edge* over men.

Men who have developed a greater level of self-control can always put themselves in a better position to bring a woman's passions to the forefront. Men must learn to *intrigue a woman's mind* more than her body. Most guys who only arouse a woman's sexual interests often become foregone conclusions.

All women need something! And no, I do not mean money. They need a *man* with the wisdom to help them ascertain their *identity*. It is a fact that *women get their identity from their fathers.* Men are the canvas on which a female can paint a wonderful portrait of femininity and grace. Like everything else in nature, *opposite qualities are always necessary for development.*

That is why I *ignore* females who say their children don't need their fathers. More often than not, women who boast this malarkey are lacking a sense of identity themselves. *Feminine strength has never been represented by aggression and independence.* It is represented by a woman's ability to be supportive and interdependent inside a healthy relationship.

Everyone in life has a *role* to play. And I for one will pass on a confused female trying to play *my* role. So often I have had to remind black women that there is no need for them to *oppose me* in the game of love.

I always have to tell them that *we are playing on the same team.* In all of Dwayne

Wade's years of playing professional basketball, I have never seen him run up to one of his teammates to *check him* when he came into the paint. Have you? *That's not what champions do!* Like LeBron, I too want to be a champion. And if the female I am with is trying to *stop me* from my goal, she can kindly kiss both soles of my Timberland's.

Even though women possess the power to *choose,* men possess the power to *oblige her choice.* As black men we already have a multiplicity of opposition challenging us. The last thing we need is a *Delilah* in our bed.

No matter what, we must not forget this society's loathing for *strong black men.* Proud black men are an anomaly in Amerikkka. Most whites in particular do not respond well to black men who are *proud to be "Black."* They feel

threatened by it.

But never let that stop you from

expressing your *manhood* every chance you get.

The *essence of manhood* also requires you to be

assertive and direct in what you want out of life.

Real men never scratch their heads unless it

itches and they never dance to a song unless

they like it.

It is also important that you learn to keep

everything in perspective. The matrix of society

is always trying to remind it's general citizenry of

their inadequacies. No matter how hard you

work, there is always someone with a bigger

house or more expensive car or prettier wife.

For many of us, *competition* has become

one of the main social pillars holding up society.

Such a destructive element often causes people to *measure* their success by the achievements of others. Men must be able to secure their positions in life and never allow envy or greed to cause them to forfeit their happiness. In other words, *men must know exactly what they want.* I once heard a saying, which says, "Life is not about getting what you want." "It's about wanting it *after* you get it!"

So many people desire to have the finer things in life but have yet to decide the *reason why* they want them. Once a man knows *why* he wants something, he can better avoid the trap of always *needing something new* to feel accomplished. Success is like crack cocaine. The more you get, the greater the *need* to get more. That is why *knowing what you want* is

more important than just chasing some *dream*
that somebody *sold* you.

And be charitable! Once *real men* achieve
their goals they can in-turn help others to
achieve their's. Luke 16:19 says: "Here's the
lesson: Use your worldly resources to benefit
others and make friends." "Then, when your
earthly possessions are gone, they will welcome
you to an eternal home." But who will welcome
a man to an eternal home when everything he
has accomplished required him to step on other
people's heads?

God did not intend for us to be *competitive*
and stressed-out about anything. Most people
in the west are always in a *rush* to go nowhere.
People who are *competitive* often suffer from
great *highs* and *lows* in life. Such drones can

never *rest*, because everything they do is based on stupid competition.

Instead, you should learn to *plan your work and work your plan.* If you work to achieve the goals you have written down on paper, who is there for you to compete with? Who would even know what you have written down as a goal in the first place? Most *machines* who are racing through life will never find true happiness. You are better than they are. Know it!

And finally, if a man ever expects to be taken seriously, he must conjure for himself a chief aim. Why would any woman get with a man without a plan? *The most important thing any man can do is sit quietly, decide what he wants, and write it down.* Every man must possess in his mind a definite vision of where he

sees himself in the next year, five years, and so
forth.

Then, he must diligently *work* to achieve
it. Otherwise, his hopes of snagging a *queen* to
place on his team will always escape him.
Remember, if a *male* has no specific place to *go*,
every mature *woman* he approaches should just
say *no*.

THE TAO OF A PLAYA'

The time has come for you to take some serious notes. I suggest these notes be jotted down in your mental notepad so you can retrieve them at will. Whether the subject be women, game, manhood, psychology, or prophecy; there is always a right and a wrong way to deal with each. So sit back, relax, and enjoy this *ism*. We will begin this discussion with the subject of *women*.

First of all, any man can *unlock* the heart and mind of a woman. But to do this he must first have a *key*. That *key* can only be found in a man's understanding of *himself*. For instance, *how would you feel if you were a woman* and

you knew that most of the guys who holla' at
you only want one thing? *Would you give it up
so easily* knowing your *mind* and *heart* are the
furthest things from their mind?

Couple this with the fact that many guys
out here *mess with dudes, too.* And to make
matters worse, a lot of these *busters* don't even
have the common decency to warn their women
about this. That's some sucka' ass shit! So
again I ask you, if you were a *woman* in this
twisted ass world, *how would you feel?*

Any person who cannot put themselves in
another person's *shoes* will never find the *key* to
understanding. Sure, you can lie to a female
and tell her what she wants to hear. But
dishonesty is some hoe ass shit. Men who
cannot be honest with their women are

amateurs. If you weren't an amateur, *why are you lying? Real men don't hide behind lies.*

Real players don't move up in the game until they can have two or more ladies and both females know about each other. *That's the game!* Anything less than this is *weak.* Know this! Women can at least respect a man who is *honest* with them. Every man should give a woman the option of *deciding* whether she is willing to *accept him* the way he is. Lying is childish. Man up!

Of course, I'm not saying a *man* should not keep certain things to himself. Of course he should. He wouldn't be a *man* if he didn't. But you are just a *boy* if you lie about who you are. I am a *player* and my woman knows this! It can't get more *real* than that.

Unfortunately, a lot of guys these days don't know how to properly lead their families. It is difficult to get a woman to respect a man who does not act like one. As players we say these lames are *messing up the game.*

What messes up the game is when women mistake *real men* for *busters.* No real man is going to stay with a female who does not respect him as a man. Women must learn not to make the mistake of placing *all men* in the same box. The same way there are different kinds of women; there are also different classes and categories of men. You just have to know what you're dealing with.

Any female who is not ready to deal with real men should just stick with boys! Real players understand that all they need to do to know *where a woman is,* is to look at her current *choice of men.* You are who you attract!

Many females try to postulate they are *more* than they are. But we *seasoned* players know how to *read* them. This is also what makes real players such a *challenge* to most females. Most women don't want to admit there are certain guys out here who *know women better than they know themselves.* Men like this represent a serious *challenge* to women. The kind of challenge most females avoid.

Some females would rather deal with a man they have a decided *edge* over. And if that edge is not there, they will *work* to create it. This is the unwritten *game* that females often *play* on their men. It is a game of *leverage.* And it can sometimes get ugly.

Women who *lose* their men due to this *game* often go *unsuspected* of causing the relationship to sour. And since no one *suspects* them, they usually go *undetected*. If a woman loses her man because she doesn't know how to treat him *it is her fault.* And until she comes to grips with this fact, she will continue to be a *loser* in love.

Unfortunately, many black women grew up without a *real man* in the home. And of the males that stayed around, many sisters saw their mothers treat them with *little* respect.

After watching your mother show little respect for black men growing up, why would you as a grown woman feel compelled to show respect for them? This society is *determined* to stamp a decrepit image of the black man in everyone's mind.

This is the black man's *reality* in Amerikkka. But this is not the black man's *truth*. The *truth is* the black man can become just as *great* as any man who understands "The Science of Greatness." Once a man understands this *science*, he can become as *great* as he allows the God within to become.

The main purpose of this book is to give its readers the key to *greatness*. Greatness cannot be achieved through the accumulation of money. Although Jim Morrison had a long run of success, Morrison never achieved *greatness*. Greatness also cannot be achieved by becoming world famous. Janis Joplin was as well connected as any person you could think of; but because Janis lacked this *key*, she failed to become *great*.

Greatness can only be attained by understanding the scripture *John 10:14.* "Jesus answered them, Is it not written in your law, I said, *Ye are gods?*" People who lack this understanding will probably believe it is blasphemous to suggest that a man can become *a god.* At no time in Jesus's life did he say he was here to do the will of himself. What made Jesus *a god* was that he understood the key to greatness is *obedience (Luke 22:42).*

Any man or woman can become *great.* The key is to learn how to submit your will to the will of the *Father.* Then, when you speak, it will be the *Father speaking through you.* When you achieve, it will be the *Father achieving through you.* Man will always come up short in his own understanding. But if he will only learn to *obey* the *still small voice of God* within him, he will undoubtedly become *great.*

Over the entrances of the great Temples in Kemet rested the words: "Man Know Thyself." The reason this is so important is because there is no way you can know anything without first having *knowledge of self.*

The same *key* that will open the door to understanding a woman will open the door to whatever you may want. The main reason I asked, *how you would feel,* is because this question will unlock many of life's most perplexing questions.

Knowing how you would *feel* in another person's shoes will give you deeper insight into the psychology of men. For instance, knowing the psychology of *white aggression* in this country will save you a lot of disappointments. Black men are the most *feared* men on the planet. Many of the reasons for this have already been discussed and *proven* time and again. So, instead of me going into an in depth explanation of this, I will just say that whenever a man aggresses another man without *probable cause,* he is acting out of *fear.*

As you should know, man is both part animal and part man. Many people who study systems involving the Chakras understand there are seven main Chakras. What they don't seem to understand is that most *westerners* are governed by their *lowest three.* The first Chakra governs *instinct, sex and survival.* The main reason this is considered the *first* Chakra is because it is also the *lowest* on the scale of vibration.

Most white people in Amerikkka are governed by the element of *competition.* This element was systematically imposed into the social structure of the society. This is the reason people are so *competitive* in this country. The only problem with this element is that it causes people to *vibrate* at their *lowest* Chakra.

"The Root Chakra" as it is called is what governs all *animal* life. Although man has the potential to vibrate at higher levels, most Americans are polarized in their *lower animal nature.* When those *four animals* killed James Craig Anderson in Mississippi, they were acting out of their *lower animal nature.*

Whenever an *animal* attacks a man, it is governed by *animal fear*. Just because a man can stand upright does not mean he is a *man*. That word can only be applied to people who are governed by a higher apparatus within their Chakra system. The same goes for those *animals* that killed Emmitt Till. In fact, the reason the Klu Klux Klan was created was to protect white interests resulting from *animal fear*. Any time you seek to postulate *supremacy* over another human being, you are being governed by your "Root Chakra."

You will often hear me say that many whites in Amerikkka are *devils*. What I mean by this is that many of them are *governed by animal fear*. As I understand it, a *devil* is the *opposite* of God. If *God is love* and the opposite of love is *fear,* then those people who are governed by fear are *devils*. Even the Bible says that <u>God did not give his children the spirit of fear.</u> This fact is irrefutable!!

God wants *his children* to have whatever they set their minds to. He wants *us* to be rich and successful because the more rich and successful *we* are the more God can express himself through us. And as I lamented earlier in this chapter, *greatness* can only come by *submitting your will* to the will of the Father.

But there is something to be said about *which path* one takes to gain riches. God does not want *his children* to earn their wealth through the *competitive process.* He wants them to get it through the *creative process.* One process leads man down the path of demonic activity. The other process leads man up the path to God.

We must accept that God did not create anything through the *competitive* process. He created everything through the *creative* process. And this is the best way to tell whether a person is *a child of God.*

God's children do not create laws that only benefit them. They would never *systematically* house certain groups of people in impoverished reservations. They would never *prejudge* anyone *they do not know.* God's children would never pass out stimulus checks to certain groups of people while overlooking everybody else. And *God's children* would *never* take part in the enslavement or *genocide* of black people in any way shape or form. *That is only the work of the devil and of his children.*

Black people who wish to *come out of the virgin daughter of Babylon* must rebuke the competitive approach to attaining wealth. If you find yourself ever feeling *anxious*, it is only because you have lost sight of *God's way.* Anxiety is just another form of fear. And fear of any kind is against the *spirit of God.*

All you have to do is know what you want and have a *definite picture of success* in your mind. To attain your image of success, you do not need to *wait* on its manifestation. You must *walk in it now!* That is the only way you will ever receive it. *Knowing what you want and walking in it* will keep you from being pulled back into the demonic cage of *competitive activity.*

People who are *anxious* or are *always in a rush* don't have control over their lower animal nature. They are what the Bible refers to as the *swine* of the earth. And according to the Bible, *you should never waste your time trying to get pigs to act like men.* The best thing you can do is leave *pigs* to their slop. You and I are *superior to them!!!*

Never again allow your thoughts to drift to inadequacy or limit. The white man has defined *economics* in Ameriikkka the wrong way. In this country, the study of economics is the *study of scarcity.* This is erroneous because it plants the seeds of limitation and lack in your subconscious mind.

The real reason Amerikkka went into Iraq was not because of weapons of mass destruction. That was the *little white lie* the government used to get your ass over there. The reason we went into Iraq was because of the white man's misunderstanding of economics. We went into Iraq for one thing and for one thing only – *oil.*

When the European believes that he's starting to get *low* on a *limited resource,* he'll do anything to get his hands on more. Even if that means killing innocent men, women, and children. He doesn't care about human life!

If he understood God gave man an *unlimited resource* to solve all of his problems, whitey would not need to *war* as often as he does. This warmongering so often perpetuated by the white man is *proof* that he is only *vibrating* at the lowest Chakra. If the white man were vibrating at his *fourth Chakra (the heart)* war would be the furthest thing from his mind.

If he had *love,* the white man would know that all he needs to solve Amerikkka's *limited resource* problem is to make full use of the *unlimited resource of his mind.* In other words, he would use the *creative process* for building wealth rather than the *competitive* one.

The Bible says that "The *meek* shall inherit the earth." Being *meek* does not mean being *docile* or *passive.* In truth, it refers to *playa's* that are humble enough to align themselves with universal law. Don't follow the path the white man has set. *Relax!* Everything that is happening with the Amerikkkan economy has already been prophesied.

Whenever there is major turmoil erupting in a world economy, it means wealth is being transferred from the arrogant to the meek! Don't fear the changes that are coming. *Relax!* So long as you align yourself with "The Tao of A Playa," you will be on God's side.

ESSENTIALS TO MACKIN'

Real men never blame others for their mistakes. So often, I hear men complaining about what happens to them as if they had *no role to play* in it. Men who feel this way are not men; they are *boys masquerading as men.*

As a player in the game of life, I realize it is my responsibility to *choose* what is best for me. By *choosing* to be with a woman that can never find fault with herself, I am putting my pimpin' in a compromising position. Whenever a relationship fails, *both parties* involved are at least as responsible. If a black female's *mirror* only works when she's checking to see if her *white girl flow* is proper, I'm uninterested. The only way to grow and mature is to do a thorough examination of your*self*.

Everyone has lessons to learn in life. As long as we are in the land of the living we still have more to learn. There is no perfect woman anymore than there is a perfect man. Perhaps the poem; "What are little boys and girls made of" has gotten a lot of females *twisted* out here. At this stage of my life, I refuse to waste my time or a dime on a dumb female. I need a mature and *psychologically stable* woman who recognizes *we are on the same team*. I mean, is that too much to ask? If there are lessons we both need to learn in a relationship, we should be learning them *together.*

As a black man living in a demonic racist society, I must stay on my Ps and Qs at all times. There are already too many secret traps and hidden craters set-up for me to fall into. Why would any self-respecting black man fight for his respect in the world and then come home to fight with a quarrelsome black woman? I need a *teammate* who understands that every team has a *team captain.* So often people want to be captains, but haven't yet learned how to be good followers.

I am not about to waste my precious time with a so-called *teammate* who doesn't understand that we are wearing the *same jersey.* If you don't know how to play this game why are you on the court? Looks like you'll be *sitting on the bench* for the rest of this season!! Relationships are tough. That's why black men must learn how to pick the right people to partner with.

A good teammate can often see issues the leader may not. The question all leaders must ask themselves is, *does my teammate have my back* or not? As an entrepreneur, I need a partner who *understands* the reason I am working so hard is so I can make our lives better. And for me to accomplish this, I must put a considerable amount of my time into my work.

As a man and as a businessman, I am going to make mistakes. In many cases, making mistakes is the only way to *know* whether something will work or not. At the same time, good leaders learn how to *hedge* themselves against potential mistakes. A good businessman can't afford to take the kind of chances that may wind up putting his family out on the street.

Men have to be sharp. They cannot afford to *throw the dice* and risk losing their home or maybe even the shirt off their back. So, even when mistakes are made, good leaders must learn to *benefit* from them. A good phrase to remember is that *mistakes are resources.* They are resources because they contain untapped knowledge. Just like a nut inside of a hard shell. Sometimes leaders have to crack their heads a little to get to the knowledge they may be lacking. Then they can say: *now I know what doesn't work!*

But there is another point I must add to this scenario. While, you must learn from your experiences in life, you cannot do so without a comprehensive understanding of universal law. It is universal law that reminds us that many of the bumps and bruises we experience are in fact *self-inflicted.*

For instance, many young men think they're invincible. They think their youth and strength are enough to *push* their way through life. But in many cases, all most young hot heads end up creating for themselves is *hard times.* It usually takes men until the ages of 40 to 45 before they start learning how to *work smarter* rather than *harder.* And although hard work is good; smart work is always better.

For instance, many people have heard the saying that *you will reap in accordance to your sowing.* What this means ultimately is that you will only get out of life what you put into it. It wasn't until I got older that I understood that *what you put into life* is also the *thoughts* that you harbor.

There is a metaphysical phrase that says: "Thoughts are things!" What this means is there are states of consciousness within ourselves where *we create* our own *experiences.* By not understanding this universal principle, we often create experiences in our lives that we don't want. That is why you will hear me repeat time and again in this book the importance of learning how to *take control of your own thoughts, moods, and feelings.*

Unfortunately, we live in a society full of *haters*. All haters want to do is take away the power that certain people have to write their own destinies. Haters are *vampires* who feed on the energy of the *children of light*. Black people must learn to be more aware of the *energy* that certain people harbor. Many racist devils in Amerikkka possess an *evil eye energy* that is only designed to *drain you* of your life force. Pay attention the next time you are around certain people. You may notice that certain people leave you feeling *depleted* of your energy. That's because these people are *energy vampires* and are not *human* even if they appear to be.

Vampires never bring positive energy. In fact, it is impossible for them to *add* to your essence in a positive way. All that *energy vampires* do is leech off the god force in others.

If you find that you live with, work with, or live near vampires, it is essential that you master the *kemetic art of protection.*

When I say Kemet, I mean the place that white invaders of North Afrika later renamed *Egypt.* The Black people who lived before Afrika was invaded did not refer to themselves as Egyptians. Ancient Egypt was called names such as, Punt or Kemet. Kemet means *people of the Black Land or Land of the Black people.*

In the ancient temple of Seti 1 in Abydos, there is no question how the Kemetian people saw themselves. On the hieroglyphs in this particular temple, the so-called "Egyptian people" painted a picture of themselves as being just as dark as the Ethiopian or Kushite people.

And just in case you don't know, Kush means,
Sunburnt!

So, when I talk about using ancient
Kemetic arts, I'm talking about what Europeans
often refer to as ***Black Magic!*** The reason Black
Magic is called *black* is because it is the most
powerful shit out there! Not because there is
anything *evil* about it. Remember, *black never
meant evil until the white man started rewriting
history to fit his own little ideal self.*

A good practice is to first learn to sit
quietly in solitude with no disturbances. Then,
imagine you are sitting or standing right in the
center of a long white rectangle. The long white
rectangle symbolizes a *protective energy field.* It
is designed to protect you from those who wish
to *feed* on your essence.

This practice is *mental.* There are no candles or anything that you have to burn or light. You are simply using the power of your own mind to manifest whatever you are in need of. Just as there are people who are *not aware* of their vampire tendencies, there are some others who are. And those who are *aware* are the most dangerous. That is why I stress the importance of learning how to *control your own thoughts, moods, feelings, and energy.*

You do not have to remain an *innocent little sheep* waiting for the next vampire to steal your essence. Take action! Master the *art* of self-protection. After doing this for a while, you will eventually come up with your own mental techniques. Learning to protect yourself on a spiritual level is one of the most important techniques you will ever master.

Like all great basketball teams, *great* men and women must develop good offense and defense. You've got to be proficient at both ends of the basketball court. Black people must develop a *passion to have more* than the world thinks they should have. And at the apex of this passion should be the strong desire to be *great*.

The main purpose of this book is to give its readers the key to *greatness*. Greatness cannot be achieved through the accumulation of money. Although John Belushi was considered the greatest comic voice of his generation, John never achieved *greatness*. Greatness also cannot be achieved by becoming world famous. Brad Renfro was as well-connected as any person you could think of; but because Brad lacked this *key*, he failed to become *great*.

Greatness can only be attained by understanding the scripture *John 10:14.* "Jesus answered them, Is it not written in your law, I said, *Ye are gods?*" People who lack this understanding will probably believe it is blasphemous to suggest that a man can become *a god.* At no time in Jesus's life did he say he was here to do the will of himself. What made Jesus *a god* was that he understood the key to greatness is *obedience (Luke 22:42).*

Any man or woman can become *great.* The key is to learn how to submit your will to the will of the *Father.* Then, when you speak, it will be the *Father* speaking through you. When you achieve, it will be the *Father* achieving through you. Man will always come up short in his own understanding. But if he will only learn

how to *listen* to the *still small voice* of God within him, he will undoubtedly become *great.*

In truth, the reason my business partner James and I have contributed to the writing of this book is because we want to help others. We want to do our part in the evolution of God's people. Although the war we face is *spiritual*, there are fundamental principles we must all master.

The Creator saw fit to preserve James' life, despite the fact that he stared down the barrel of a gun on more than one occasion. In this book, James and I have a lot to share with you. We have chosen to deliver these *gifts* of knowledge in one dynamic philosophical presentation.

James and I are not writing this book because we are so smart, but because God has a greater plan for our lives. As we impart our combined understanding, we are humbled by the fact there is a greater power at work in the universe. We don't care what you call it as long as you have the intelligence to recognize it. Experience has taught us that *wisdom* is the best teacher. Many people believe that *experience* is the best teacher. But so often, experience is the *hardest* teacher.

If *wisdom is the proper application of knowledge,* then you don't have to bump your head against the wall to learn what not to do. *You can simply research how to do it the right way the first time.* So many people make the mistake of diving into situations without doing adequate research beforehand. In the Bible it refers to this as *counting the cost before you build!*

That is why I say that *wisdom is the best teacher and experience is the hardest.* All of us must learn to make full use of this brain God has given us. The left hemisphere of the brain is used for logistics and fact gathering. The right hemisphere is used for coming up with creative anecdotes to solve problems. And finally, the subconscious mind is used for the *metaphysical.* Many people have a desire to accomplish a goals but are not making full use of their brain capacity.

By far, the greatest influence in your life is your subconscious mind. This is where your deepest beliefs and thoughts about yourself and the world are played out. If you set a goal in your left brain and conjure up creative ways to achieve that goal in your right brain; the number one factor affecting your ability to achieve it lies in your subconscious mind.

Subconscious or intuitive activity is the number one factor separating the rich from the poor. Rich people attract wealth on a regular basis because they have learned how to *program* their intuitive minds for success. Poor people attract poverty on a regular basis because their inner minds are *programmed* to attract privation. That is why it is so important for the "Establishment" to keep black people trapped in impoverished reservations. They understand that by surrounding black people with destitution and few opportunities, they can program us to attract poverty on an intergenerational level.

In most European's research related to *black academic and social achievement,* whites often postulate that our inability to excel in these areas is due to a *genetic deficiency.* When the fact is, *rich elites* set up the game for black and poor people to fail. If you want more proof, simply *research the academic and social achievements of poor white trash* and see if you find any major differentials.

Even a devil behind closed doors will admit *there is no separation between genetic and environmental influences.* The only problem with these *facts* is that I'm not supposed to be *intelligent* enough to articulate them. Now, maybe you're beginning to see why it was so important for the white man to keep black people *illiterate* on his plantation.

You see, *knowledge* has the power to redirect your consciousness. By not giving the black man the *human right* to read and educate himself, the white man was better able to control him. *No human being would even try to justify the enslavement of black people.* And no human being would support the *privileges they now enjoy* as a result of such malevolent behavior. You are a *wicked* and *malevolent* person if you fall into either one of these two categories!

The most important discipline black men must master is to *think for themselves*. Even if you've made many mistakes in the past, you can *choose* to make your life better. Opportunity is imminent. The white man cannot keep you from going on the Google search engine and *educating yourself* about everything under the Sun.

Make no mistake about it; *the information age is our age!!* Most financial knowledge that was once only privy to *wealthy elites* is now available to the *whole world.* If you fail in the information age, you cannot use the tired excuse of blaming it on *the white man.* There is entirely too much internet based information available today outside Twitter and Facebook.

If you just got to *tweet* somebody, why not tweet someone who is smarter or richer than you are; someone who can *help you elevate* your consciousness. Stop wasting so much time on dumb shit that's not going to put a dime in your bank account. That is, unless, you like being poor!

Plenty of people marvel over the time they waste from day-to-day. So much of what people *could do* is erroneously put off until some later date. The problem with putting off important tasks is that it often creates a negative snowball effect. Jim Rohn once defined success as: "A few simple disciplines practiced everyday." According to Jim, success comes as a result of tackling *all the little tasks* on our to–do lists. It's so easy to put off small tasks until a more *favorable* time. A good thought to remember is that *everything you do affects everything else.*

By not knocking out simple tasks you invariably affect your motivation in a negative way. Once your motivation has been stunted, you will lack the *desire* to check off many of the other tasks you will need to accomplish. The result of this lag in motivation is a person who spends most of his time *explaining* rather than *celebrating.*

A good movie to watch that shows the utter importance of making full use of your time is: "In Time," starring singer Justin Timberlake. In this movie, people use the *time* they have left to live to buy things or pay their bills. The rich, who have an almost unlimited amount of time to live, get richer because they are *selling* the products and services that poor and middle class people need. The more the middle class patronize the rich, the less time they have to pay for things and live.

This movie shows clearly the wealth distribution levels between the *rich* and *everybody else.* People who have more money can buy more time to live because they can afford better health care. They can also put themselves in a position to *sell time* to the poor and middle class.

Whenever a person pays their rent or mortgage, they are *buying time.* You are not buying a home when you pay your mortgage. You are only *buying 30 more days* to stay there. The house is not *yours* until you burn the mortgage. The same principle goes for paying a car note.

People need to understand this concept of *buying* and *selling time.* The same idea relates to paying insurance, renting to own furniture and appliances, or even paying a prostitute or stripper for their *services.* If you are *buying time* from someone that must mean they are *selling you time.*

Essentially, every monthly *expense* you pay is *income* for somebody else. As you can see, even if everyone was given the same amount of money to work with, some people would

maneuver themselves into a position to *sell time*

to everyone else. And that is how the rich get

richer and richer as time *ticks* on.

The question you must ask yourself is *how*

can I begin a life of selling time? And once you

answer that question, your next question should

be *how can I sell time to others without needing*

to be present to get paid? The first question will

give you a good idea on how to become self-

employed. The second question will give you a

vision of how you can turn your small enterprise

into a real business.

A real business is defined as an entity that

makes money for you without you. When you are

ready to take your business to the next level,

you will need to begin the process by hiring

competent people. The positions you will be looking to fill will be both for workers and advisers who can help point you and your business in the right direction. As I said in my first book: "Milkk" on Amazon.com, *an independent hustler is a broke ass hustler.*

People who wish to succeed in business will have to partner up with other people who are talented, focused, ambitious, and a team player. A real business cannot afford to have different egos all fighting for the same positions in the company. That's why it is essential that every member have a *different* job to do. That way, no one will have any business meddling in the affairs of others. This will help to keep down unnecessary drama so everybody can *focus* on what they are supposed to be doing.

Although one mind can come up with great ideas on how to best sell time to others; multiple minds can come up with even more. The other benefit of establishing a *real business* for yourself is that you will be acting within the laws of the universe.

Reciprocity is a law that deals with the principle of being blessed because of blessing others. Many self-employed people are *selfish* because they only create a job for *themselves*. But the universe rewards those who also create jobs for others. People need to start with a *grand vision* of their business. This grand vision will enable them to help others help themselves.

Apart from the product or service you are providing, you must also think about ways you can create jobs for others. People who don't understand this principle often find themselves *lacking* in their blessings. The wisest leaders not only work to create jobs for others but they also pay their people well.

If you can take the time and energy to think of a worthy business to start, you can also use that same energy to create a grand enough plan that includes the *services* of others. That way, when it comes time for you to *harvest,* you will have a *blessing* that you alone won't have room for.

With the current state of our economy, it is obvious the middle class is being wiped-out. That leaves America with only *two classes of people,* the rich and the poor. It's sad that most people still haven't learned to make full use of the many lessons in history. Far too many people blindly trust *someone else* to take care of them when they are no longer able to take care of themselves.

For instance, how many people in America understand that Social Security is nothing more than a huge Ponzi scheme? The money that is paid to retirees when they retire is not coming from the pool of money they paid into during their years of employment.

The money paid to retirees comes from the pool of money the current working class is paying into. But with all the jobs in America being given to the Chinese and Indian people, it should be obvious to you there may not be enough people working in America to pay into the pot from which your retirement income will be drawn.

That is why the number one fear of Americans is not having enough money to live on when they retire. Not to mention, *Medicare is not guaranteed* to be around for anybody. Even if politicians lie and say they can guarantee it, they have no more control over Medicare than real estate brokers have over the ups and downs of real estate.

The thing you must remember about all politicians, all real estate brokers, all stockbrokers, all insurance salesmen, and all preachers is that they are all *salesmen*. And a salesman is never as concerned with the *validity of his promises* as much as he is with his *commission$*. May the *church* say, Amen?

Now understand, I am not saying being a salesman is a bad thing. On the contrary! Sales in the highest paid profession there is. And if you intend to do well in life or in business, you had better learn how to *sell*. With that said, you still need to know whether what someone is selling you is best for you. Otherwise, you will just be another sucker waiting for some slick salesman to *sell you* on something.

America is the largest debtor (borrowing) nation in the world. China is the largest creditor (lending) nation in the world. So I wouldn't put too many of my eggs in America's economic basket. That is why smart Americans are starting to purchase gold and silver coins as a way to hedge the falling value of the dollar.

At the time of this writing, you can go to your local coin seller and purchase silver coins for under $40. Silver at this *low price* is a steal because unlike gold, silver is a *consumable* commodity. What this means is that every new phone, computer, and gadget has *silver* in it. Therefore, the more they create new electronic devices for you to buy, the less silver there is in the earth.

And as it goes with all dwindling commodities in the earth, the *value* of it will one day skyrocket. My goal here is to *sell you* on the importance of getting your hands on a nice amount of pure silver *before* it becomes in serious demand. This is just a little *tip* from us for you and your family to consider.

If there's one thing my partner James learned in the United States Army is that many men are *pussies*. Many men who seem to be strong willed and focused often *fold* under pressure. For instance, most white men in Amerikkka are not strong enough to deal with the *around the clock pressures* that come with being black. They would all throw in the towel soon, if not sooner.

This proves that black men are naturally stronger than most other races of men. Whites may know how to *dish out the hate,* but they will never understand what it is like to deal with their malevolence *24 hours a day.* From the *constant evil stares* to their most obvious signs of aggression and judgment, *I'd love to see how strong these haters really are. Just 24 hours* of dealing with their own *fears* and *insecurities* would be enough to tell the story.

Black men who intend to become prominent in Amerikkka must first and foremost learn to count on themselves. All *opportunity* begins in your *thoughts.* You've got to develop a grand vision of yourself; a vision that you hold in your mind's eye. Prejudice and hatred will always exist as long as man remains on this *low level of vibration.* So, either you learn to deal with it as *a god* or you allow yourself to get swallowed up by it.

When I write about the way many whites in Amerikkka *see* black men, it is not to cause you to *hate* them. Remember, "Whatever you hate you tie yourself to." There is no reason you should be *tied to someone* if they are already mindlessly tied to you.

Hating white people will only pull you down to a low level of vibration. Leave hate to

The Science of Greatness   137

those who are proficient at hating. <u>You are</u>
<u>above that!</u>

Instead, *fall in love with yourself and with*
your goals! True love is stronger than hate.
Refocus your attention on *what you want* rather
than on *what you don't want.* The universe can
either be your *friend* or your *foe.* Let it work for
you rather than against you. And another
important note to consider. You cannot be a
winner in the world of business and commerce
without *credit.*

Many people who don't understand "The
Essentials To Mackin" will tell you that *debt is*
bad. Not true. There are two kinds of debt.
Good debt and bad debt. Bad debt is when you
use credit to *floss* rather than to *invest.*
Examples of bad debt are using credit cards to

purchase things that you can't sell later for more money than you paid for it. A $200,000 car will immediately lose *$75,000 of its value* the second you pull it off the lot. No matter how pretty the car may be, this is still *bad debt*.

Good debt is using a line of credit to invest in something that will *return you a profit*. When Donald Trump builds a new building, he's not using his own money to do it. He's using the bank's money. If you need to establish credit for yourself, you may have to start out small.

Go to a major credit card company and fill out there *Secured Credit Card application.* This will give you a start in building credit for yourself. For people who have bad credit, I strongly recommend *rebuilding your credit* in this way. Folks, if you are not on the *inside* of the game, you are on the *outside.* You got to have credit in this world if you intend to do things in a big way.

And a word of advice on credit use: *never swipe your credit card unless you already have the cash to pay it back.* Remember, you only have 30 days! The key to debt is 1) Don't purchase a bunch of *stuff* you can't make *mo' money* with. And 2) Never get overextended. Getting overextended is when you spend more in a single month than you can *comfortably* pay back in a month's time. Follow these few simple rules and you will be well on your way to a new and prosperous life.

And one final thought on being a *real player. If you want to be a player, you got to find a soulmate!* This *soulmate* represents a person who has the *right energy* for you. People often think of *their soulmate* as a person with all the right personality characteristics needed for wealth building and achievement. No, the right man or woman for you is the person with the *right energy.* This is the *secret* to achieving at your highest level.

You cannot exceed the level and quality of the people you link yourself with. This principle is the hidden secret to your success. It is what is known as the "Master Mind" principle. A "Master Mind" is what is created because of two or more dynamic minds coming together in the interest of one.

Whenever two or more dynamic minds come together, they create a *third mind* that has more power than any one mind all by itself.

Once a "Master Mind" is created, doors that were once *closed* will just *open up.* The key to taking advantage of the "Master Mind" principle is to never allow yourself to become conceited in believing that *you* alone are responsible for your success.

So often, arrogance kills a 'Master Mind" causing the entire conglomerate to dissolve. And once a good team is *separated by ego,* all the *benefits* that came as a result of that team are lost. Remember, the *first thing Jesus did* before he started his ministry was put together a "Master Mind" principle in the form of *disciples.*

Sometimes, it's not a particular *set of skills* that makes certain people *invaluable* to an organization. But rather, it's the *energy* they bring to the table. When you are finally linked-up with the right partner you will catapult yourself to heights you once only dreamed of achieving.

Success at the highest level is always the result of a "Master Mind." Although an *individual* may achieve at high levels; it's only after he unites with the *right team* can he become a champion!

STEP YO' GAME UP!

Although *vision* is essential to your success, no playa' can master "The Science of Greatness" without good human relations. As much as men *rap* about being *players*, most of them have no understanding about the true nature of women. Since I was blessed with a certain level of charisma, maybe I'm taking what comes naturally to me for granted. I still think that men today could at least make a better effort to *learn from their past mistakes*. To me, too much of what men do, as it relates to women is more of a cliché than something *real*.

143

Good examples are men who talk too loud or try to appear *strong* so women will notice them. These tactics may get you noticed, but they will probably be counterproductive. Although, the Bible suggests *no man understands the ways of a woman*; I happen to be one of those men who do.

The key to understanding women is found in learning to understand your *feminine side.* Men who are heterosexual often claim they don't have a feminine side – but they do. The feminine part of man is his *emotional* side. Too often men have been told not to express their emotions, but that doesn't mean they don't have any. By understanding your emotions better, you will be better able to relate to women.

Women need more than just a strong man to help them carry the mattress and dresser up the stairs. Sometimes they just need a man who knows how to *sit quietly* and *listen*. Knowing how to do this, is good as gold. Women are talkers. And the man who can get females to *open up* to him is always going to attract women. Another quick secret for men is that women need a man who knows how to allow himself to be *touched* and *moved* by what moves them.

This may take some time, but men have to learn how to communicate to women that they are at least trying to understand *the way they feel*. It doesn't mean you will always understand, but at least you can make her *feel* like you're trying.

Any man who has ever lived with a woman knows how important it is for her to *feel happy*. Whenever a woman feels upset or neglected *you will know it* because the entire *atmosphere* of your home will change. And after a while, you will find yourself rifling through your memory bank to find the *source* of her discontentment. But in many cases, *just learning to listen to your woman* could help you keep your home's atmosphere *peaceful.* And I have yet to meet a man who doesn't understand the importance of having *peace of mind* in his home.

In the dating game, men need to understand that women are *visual* creatures. You don't want to ruin your chances of being *chosen* by being corny. One of the first things women do when observing a man is to look at his *shoes.* They may even ask each other: *What shoes was he rocking?* You may be a nice guy but if your shoes look *crusty* you are well on your way to being forgotten.

If you can't afford *new* shoes, always keep your old ones clean. If you want to build a 100 story building, you first have to lay a *foundation* strong enough to hold 100 stories. Your shoes are that foundation. Next, examine your wardrobe and overall style. What does your dress code say about you? Or better yet, what do you want it to say? You may have to think about this for a while, but trust me; *if you don't look the part you are trying to play,* you will be eliminated from consideration altogether.

An easy way to start this process is to first find something about yourself that is unique. Perhaps you have a nice smile. Perhaps women like your handsome face. Whatever it may be, try to organize your wardrobe around that. In every hand dealt, there are strong and weak cards. Your goal is to examine your own hand and concentrate on those cards which best represent your strengths. If you are unsure about where to start, maybe you could ask a *female friend* to give you a good lookin'-over. Once you can ascertain one or more positive qualities about yourself, you must then work to arrange your wardrobe to magnify those qualities. But whoever you get to help you, make sure they have their stuff together.

Next, say it with your style. Style as you know is your unique way of expressing your individuality. The main reason this is important is so you don't make the mistake of dressing just like the store mannequin. You need your own style! So try this, what two words best describe your personality?

If I had to choose two words to describe me, it would be *Kooool* & *Pimpish*. The *Kooool* part speaks to my core personality traits. In fact, one woman named me *Kooool breeze,* because she said she can almost feel a cool breeze flow by her when I come around. So, *Kooool* represents about 75 percent of my *swag*. The second word, *pimpish*, describes the distinct way I express my charisma. There are all kinds of *players* in the world. My particular way is to be *quietly confident but always in control.* And I never walk fast. I takes my time.

Now, pick two words to describe *you*. The first word should describe the largest aspect of your personality. The second word should describe some creative or interesting side of you.

Perhaps you enjoy reading or intellectual conversation. If so, find a nice pair of designer frames to give you that *sexy teacher look.* Perhaps, a special haircut or style of suit could best convey your second personality trait. I am not trying to define *your* characteristics here. That is your bag. I am simply trying to give you some *good ideas* to help you *$ell* yourself. And remember, the sooner you get started on this process – the better.

Another thing to consider in this process is *color.* Simply put, colors have meaning. So, your first goal is to understand the meanings behind every color. Then, you must add the appropriate colors to your wardrobe. For instance, red symbolizes *action, confidence, courage and vitality.* While brown symbolizes *earth, order, and convention.*

A person who has a more down-to-earth easy-going personality might want to add more browns to his wardrobe. While a person who is more intellectually oriented might want to try variations of yellow. Yellow represents *wisdom, joy, happiness, and intellectual energy.* Some other colors and their meanings are pink, which represents *love and beauty;* orange, which represents *vitality, endurance and healing;* and finally green, which represents *life, nature, fertility and well-being.*

If you are seeking further assistance with putting your wardrobe together you can always subcontract my services. I do have a good reputation for great style. If you are interested in doing business with me please give me a holler. Good luck!

But remember, *beauty is always in the eye of the beholder.* You don't have to be a Tyson Beckford to pull a dime piece. All you need to do is understand your strengths and weaknesses and work to magnify your strengths. That's all! Beautiful women have been known to choose men they admittedly *were not attracted* to at first. If the Notorious B.I.G. can pull Faith Evans and Lil Kim there is hope for all of us. Know this!

Now that you've gotten yourself fashionably together, it's time for you to work on *carrying yourself in the right way.* A key to carrying yourself properly is to always remember

that *men are smooth and women are graceful.*
Even if you are a high-energy person, you still
want to represent your *gender* qualities in the
proper way.

For instance, I happen to be riding
through the hood, when my eyes fell upon a sexy
young *shorty.* I'm interested! And just as I'm
getting ready to see if the eye contact is there,
she cocks, leans over and *spits* onto the ground.
Cave bitch! The only thing left for a pimp to do is
to *mash the gas and speed past her nasty ass.*
Who told these broads that this shit is
attractive? A woman is supposed to be *graceful*
not brutish. Even, if I was pimping and she was
my hoe; that would not be acceptable.

On the flip side, are men who are way too
rough around the edges. I have known men who

were attractive guys, but who turned women off by not knowing how to be *smoother* with their shit. I mean saying stuff like how big their dick is in the first half hour of a conversation – *come on bleed.* When dudes do dumb stuff like this, it makes true players like me feel embarrassed. I do not want to be associated with lames who do not know how to properly carry themselves. At least for me, women were always able to tell that I was much smoother than the bad company I sometimes kept.

Women are like felines. They *purr* when you rub them the right way. But they'll *scratch the shit out of you* if you scare them or back them into a corner. So learn to be smooth instead of clumsy or too forthcoming. It's hard enough for black men as it is.

And then there's the *give-and-take technique.* Now, I'm getting ready to get into some real pimp shit, so you might want to write some of this down. The *give-and-take technique* is when a man *gives* a woman affection to show her that he is, *affectionate.* But then, he *balances* that affection with a certain level of *distance.* The *give-and-take technique* is a man's way of balancing love and toughness with a woman. If done correctly, it will keep a woman on her toes. The problem with many men today is that they are either *too nice* or *too hard.* They have no balance. Guys who are *too nice* are often *taken for granted* or even taken advantage of by women. Hence the phrase, "Nice guys finish last." You don't want to be tossed into that category. It will hurt your *pimpin'* for maybe the rest of your life.

And then there are those guys who are *too hard*. Most guys, who are like this, don't know or don't care how to establish a comfortable balance between *hard* and *soft*. The problem with not having both aspects with a woman is that women can and often do get *bored* with their men. If you intend to keep a woman's interest you better learn how to spice things up from time-to-time. And a side note to remember, not only can that hard crap cause you to lose the woman you love, but it can also backfire on your ass!

I have seen dudes that played *hardball* with women turn *cotton soft*. A woman *can* be conniving as hell. Remember that! In fact, some women will *intentionally* deal with a *hard* dude just to make him *soft for her*. And once she succeeds in *defeating* him, she'll *walk away* like nothing ever happened. What often follows is a string of phone calls, desperate texts, and random stop-bys from the guy trying to get some semblance that she still loves him. But nooooo. *She never did.* All he was, was a *test* of her Female Mackin' skills. Now, she's off to the next hard mutherfucker to conquer. You lames out there, better pay close attention to pimpin'. I'm giving up the grapes on this one.

In the pimp game, pimps are *100 percent mental.* How else can you explain a fine ass woman *giving all of her money* to a man? For instance, how can you explain one of my ex girlfriends making all this money and then giving me *her entire check* to manage and orchestrate the way I saw fit? You know how...? Pimpin is strong baby!!! Malcolm X understood this fact better than anyone. In fact, he once said: "Most men need to know what the pimps know." "That a woman is to occasionally be *babied*, enough to show her the man has affection." "But beyond that, she should be treated *firmly!*" What Malcolm was describing in his autobiography is none other than the *give-and-take technique.* Remember, the last thing anyone wants to be is *too predictable.*

Not too long ago, I was conversing with a male friend and his ex. We were discussing a plethora of subjects when the conversation finally turned into a discussion about male and female relationships. As the conversation progressed, my friend and his ex began to talk about *their* relationship. It was interesting. As my friend expressed his feelings, it was clear to me that he was tired of all the *games* associated with male and female relationships.

Frustrated, my friend all but *threw up his hands* at the way women treat him. He went on. As his ex and I listened intently to his closing remarks, his ex finally spoke up: "See, your main problem is that you always let women get into your head!" As I listened to what seemed like a convincing argument, I wondered whether any of this was getting through to him — it wasn't. Unfortunately, he like most *squares* would rather *blame the game* rather than wise up and *learn from it.*

No matter how tired you get with this *game of love,* I think it's time that men accepted the fact that it is indeed a *game.* Not everyone in relationships is looking for true love. Sometimes, it's just a *test.* Another statement that is often erroneously made by men who are married is that they have in effect, *laid down their playing cards forever.* Bullshit! Throwing up your fists at a television in protest against the Vietcong is a lot less dangerous than getting your ass shipped over there to fight. Men and women who are married are essentially *more on the front lines* than their single friends. The *game* doesn't stop just because some preacher pronounced you husband and wife.

To me, that's when the real shit starts... For instance, my parents have been married for over 41 *years*!! In this day and age of divorce, divorce, divorce, that's an incredible feat. Just two years ago my grandfather made the transition. He and my Granny, who is now 91, were married for *68 years*!!! *Wisdom is the proper application of knowledge.* And these days, *staying married* as long as my people have is a much greater *test* of their faith, strength, patience, tolerance, and understanding than just dating a bunch of different people.

We all need love. But love as it is erroneously called is still a *game... And if you choose not to play the game, you will lose the game by forfeit.* A main reason I call love a *game* is because in the western world, most people only understand *emotional love.* This is love that deals with *opposites.* People who only deal in *emotional love* can often go from *love* to *hate* in a matter of minutes. The main reason this is possible is because in emotional love, the feelings of *love* and *hate* are really *the same emotion.* In emotional love a wife can *love* her husband at night before she goes to bed and then *hate* him by the morning.

As we delve deeper into this subject you will find that true or *conscious love* evades most people. In emotional love, the only difference between love and hate is the way you *see* the person. But that is not real love. The next love I will talk about is known as *physical love.* Physical love takes place when a person has *strong sexual or lustful ties* to another person. A good example of this is when a woman stays in a relationship with a *boy* only because he has some *good dick!* I can't tell you how many times women have told me about finding themselves in these situations. In these instances, *intelligence, character, vision, and spirituality* had nothing to do with why they stayed. It was mainly *physical.*

And finally, there is *conscious love.* Conscious love takes place only when a spiritually evolved person has learned to *accept another person lock, stock, and barrel.* In the other two aforementioned loves, there was always a *condition needed* for them to work. But in *conscious* love, the commitment in question is *beyond condition.* A good example of this is what Christians often call *Agape Love.* This is the kind of love God has for us. But such a love cannot be achieved by the *average* person. It can only come by way of an *evolved* or fully *conscious being.* That is why it is called *conscious love.*

Another good note to remember about conscious love is that real love has more to do with *acceptance* than it does anything else. When a man or women can *accentuate their lover's virtues while allowing for their faults,* they are moving closer to *conscious love.* It would be the kind of love that the grandmother had for her husband in the movie "Soul Food." Even though her husband had a bad gambling problem, *she stayed with him* and did whatever she had to do to keep her family together. This is the kind of love we all need to be striving to achieve.

No soul mate is going to be perfect. That's why true love has to be *patient, kind, tenderhearted, bearing all things, enduring all things, forgiving all things, and believing all things.* Conscious love never fails!

Another word of importance is the word *consistency.* A man must be consistent both with whom he *says* he is and who he *proves* himself to be. People are always paying attention! You can't portray one thing over *here* and be another over *there* or you'll lose *credibility.* And without credibility you'll become *that guy* who talks a good game but never delivers on his promises. If there's one reputation you don't want, it's the reputation of being a *fake.* *Word* travels almost as fast as the Internet. And with Facebook and other social media out there, being a fraud is the last thing you want people to think about you.

Whenever a female is interested in a man, she will often ask around about him. She may even attempt to associate with some of the guy's closest friends. This is also a good way for a female to gauge a man's character. People can tell a lot about a person simply by examining the *company* that he keeps. If this seems *too thirsty* a move for her, she might just *observe* a man's closest friends from a safe distance.

Most women are particular about not playing their hand too soon. They would much rather get a dude to *play his hand first*. That way, if he's a total let down, she can nicely reject his offer and move on. Men who wish to make a favorable impression must work at being *consistent* no matter who they hang around. That way, when a *word on the street* leaks out about them, those who *know him* will know whether it is true or not.

Being consistent can only *help you get chose,* especially when the word on the street conveys certain characteristics a female might be interested in. But no matter what, always make sure you keep it real. Don't pretend to be a *player* if you're not. If you're a *square* then be a square. Never portray yourself in a different way because *game always recognizes game...*

While I cannot promise you will develop a strong Mack hand, I can at least make sure you don't make a fool of yourself. And one final thought to consider. In life it is essential *you know when to say when.* So often when guys have a nice conversation with a female, they always feel they have to ask for her number. Not true. Sometimes, it is best to just *leave it up to destiny.*

There are times when I've had a great conversation in a public place with a fine ass woman. And when the conversation was over, I had the *class* to say, *Well, it was nice talking to you, have a nice day.* The reason I do this is because I don't want to be the *third* or *fourth* guy to offer her their number. No, I want to be *the only one* who didn't. If a woman was impressed with me and is *available* the next time we cross paths, she will be *happy* to see me. Remember,

rather than being *too thirsty,* sometimes you just

have to have the wisdom to *pay it forward.*

SPIRITUAL UNDERSTANDING

Mary Magdalene understood that religion and spirituality are two different *concepts!* So often people confuse the two and use their religion as a way to *judge* those who worship God in a *different way.* God as we refer to Him is only a *concept.* The word concept means: "An *idea* of something formed by mentally combining all of its characteristics or particulars." The more we *grow* in life, the more our ideas *change* to suit our current *understanding.* All religions are a great place to begin building on these *ideas.* It is through our religious *paths* that we end with a *real and personal relationship with God.*

When James and I were first introduced to the religion of our families, we felt we had the *one true concept of God.* I was *Christian* and James was a *Jehovah's Witness.* The more our understanding *grew,* the more we learned to appreciate *all* the various ideas of God. This I think is where *spirituality* begins. Once we accepted that *none of us* has all the answers, we were better able to step away and observe the truth. *All of us are on the path!* And the second we try to judge others we immediately cut ourselves off from the essence we claim we are representing. Spirituality is more than a religion. It is an existentially growing experience.

We must learn to look *within* more than look *outside* of ourselves for true understanding.

In the beginning of our *journey* we made the same mistakes most religious zealots make; namely, using our religions as a *yardstick* to measure all others. At the time, we did not realize we were acting like the Romans who adopted Christianity and made it the *official religion* of the western world. Often, people who come into a new knowledge tend to *cast stones* at others. What the Roman Christians did not understand was their acts of *force and judgment* killed everything *Christian* about Christianity. God did not give any man the right to cast a stone at anyone. Were not the Romans the first group of people who routinely slaughtered Christians for fun on Saturday evenings?

For *growth* to take place, it is necessary for a man to *feel deeply* the concepts in question. The Romans did not adopt Christianity for *spiritual* reasons. They adopted it for *political* reasons. And as far as I am concerned there is no room for *politricks* in the Kingdom of God. To this day many religious zealots are the first people to judge others for having different belief systems. That just goes to show, that *playing the name game* doesn't necessarily convey spirituality.

This is a danger inherent in all religions; it is the creation of *division* caused by opposing religious concepts. But if you are *growing* the way you are supposed to, you will understand that your current concepts of God are going to *change.* There's no way around this. The more people argue their different concepts of God, the

harder it will be for any of them to find Him.
There is no reason two intelligent individuals
cannot discuss differing ideas and not be able to
disagree without being disagreeable.

In truth, some people are more concerned
with *being right* than they are with *being a
student.* I am a student of life and I hope you will
learn to be the same. Unfortunately, most
people are not interested in educating
themselves beyond their limited ideas of reality.
Even when certain persons have attained a
degree of knowledge, their doggedness to these
concepts keeps them stuck at the same level of
understanding.

Knowledge is like a seed. And seeds are
not meant to stay seeds. If ever a seed is
planted on fertile soil, it will *change* and become

something altogether *different.* And this is the great miracle of life – *planting seeds.* As I think about this, I am thankful the Creator did not leave us with the hard job of making trees. All He asks of us is that we become *good planters* of seeds. *If man would only make himself available to plant God's seeds, God will do the hard part of making the tree.* And since God is a God of infinite wisdom, I think this is more than a favorable arrangement.

Only the *ego* of man causes him to assume that his *planting* is more important than another's. The man who plants the tulips in *God's garden* is just as important as the man who plants the apple trees. The important fact we must remember is that *none of us own the Garden.* We are merely *sharecroppers* in it.

The more we grow, the more we will be able to help others to do the same. But the moment we become stagnant in our understanding, we limit our development. And to be stagnant in life is to be *dead*.

The main purpose of this book is to give its readers the key to *greatness*. Greatness cannot be achieved through the accumulation of money. Although Rob Pilatus had achieved success with Milli Vanilli, Rob still never achieved *greatness*. Greatness also cannot be achieved by becoming world famous. Hillel Slovak was as well-connected as any person you could think of. But because Hillel lacked this *key*, he failed to become *great*.

Greatness can only be attained by understanding the scripture *John 10:14*. "Jesus answered them, Is it not written in your law, I said, *Ye are gods?*" People who lack this understanding will probably believe it is blasphemous to suggest that a man can become *a god.* At no time in Jesus's life did he say he was here to do the will of himself. What made Jesus *a god* was that he understood the key to greatness is *obedience (Luke 22:42).*

Any man or woman can become *great.* The key is to learn how to submit your will to the will of the *Father.* Then, when you speak, it will be the *Father* speaking through you. When you achieve, it will be the *Father* achieving through you. Man will always come up short in his own understanding. But if he will only learn how to *listen* to the *still small voice* of God within him, he will undoubtedly become *great.*

Just like the famous alcoholic commercial suggests, "Stay *thirsty* my friends!" We must stay *thirsty* for greatness, knowledge, and higher levels of understanding. Never should we allow ourselves to think that our current level of understanding is the *end all, be all.* And yet, there are certain *concepts* that are ever pervasive throughout the universe.

One such set of concepts are known as the *Laws of the Universe.* These laws are principles which govern all of creation. And even though God never does anything outside of these laws, He is not subject to them. Overall, there are seven major universal laws. Christians like to call them "Kingdom Principles." These laws were first promulgated in Afrika. They are: MENTALISM, CORRESPONDENCE, VIBRATION, POLARITY, RHYTHM, CAUSE & EFFECT, and

GENDER. Although, I could take more time to elaborate on each. I would much rather simplify them to their *least common denominator.*

In a nutshell, all seven universal laws come down to *one*; the law of <u>CAUSE & EFFECT</u>. All the other laws are only different aspects of this same law. The general definition of the law of "Cause & Effect" is that *for every Cause, there is an Effect, and for every Effect, there is a Cause.* The gist of this law will help us to realize that no matter how you slice it, *people only get what they deserve in life!* The Bible speaks about a man who will *reap* in accordance to his *sowing.* We must all accept *full responsibility* for the consequences of our actions.

If anyone of you is in a bad predicament, you must first figure out *what role you played* in

creating it. People who try to avoid this
responsibility always find themselves in the
same kinds of situations time after time. Men
who *blame* their succession of bad experiences
in life on mere *luck* or *chance* are immature.

I say this because there is no such thing
as *chance.* There is only *universal law* not
recognized. Once man learns how to *use law for
his benefit,* he will invariably become a *master* of
the earth. Lazy people are prone to a life of
excuses. They blame their good or bad fortune
in life on *luck* instead of on themselves. But
there is no room in an evolved *being's* existence
for *excuses.* At some point every man must take
full responsibility for his life.

The reason schools made our desks in
kindergarten so small was so they would not *fit*

us when we turn 30. But many *adults* today act
as if they are still as *emotionally dependent* as
they were as children. A child cannot be
expected to reason and think as an adult. That
is why parents must take full responsibility for
the well being of the child. But once that child
reaches the *age of accountability*, he becomes
personally responsible for the consequences of
his actions. No *mature* adult can skate through
life *blaming others* for how his life has turned
out.

In the process of growth we will make
mistakes. The goal is to find the *resources*
inherent in our mistakes. Mistakes are great
teachers that can make us better if we learn
from them. Far too many people avoid making
mistakes. They wish for *immediate success* in
everything they do. But success is a horrible

teacher. You can't learn anything when you don't make mistakes. And often, immediate success can set you up for an even greater failure later on. Success has the power to overinflate your ego. And as the Bible laments, "Pride come just before *crash.*"

Instead of wishing for immediate success, be ready to learn the lessons inherent in your mistakes. Successful people make mistakes all the time. The only difference between a successful person and the average person is that successful people welcome mistakes.

In life we will only be a *failure* when we throw in the towel. This point also speaks to the law of "Cause & Effect." We are all the *causes* of the many *effects* in our lives. By not coming to grips with this fact most people become a failure.

Another fact that many people struggle with is it is always better to *affirm the truth* rather to *affirm a lie.* So many people think of affirmations as these positive phrases we repeat to ourselves which are supposed to create *change* in our lives. But what if the affirmation you are telling yourself is a lie? To me, if you are going to affirm anything, you might as well *affirm the truth!*

Let's say you are 40 years old and are 20 pounds overweight. For most people, they might *affirm* that they are losing weight and getting healthier day by day. The problem with this affirmation is that it could cause you to only become a mere *dreamer.*

Dreaming of losing weight will not *cause* you to make the necessary *changes* you will need to make in your life. Jesus never said that *lies would set us free*. He said the *truth will set you free*. Having the courage to *tell yourself the truth* is a great way to motivate you to make necessary changes in your life. Otherwise, you should just read another *positive* book!

Mature men and women do not run and hide from the truth. They face it! What better way to take control of your life than to deal squarely with the *reality of your situation?* And in speaking of *reality*, there is another reality we must face. That *reality* is there is a *higher power* at work in the universe. Regardless of what you call this reality, we must at some point come to grips with it. One scripture regarding this fact stands out to me. It is James 4:8, which says

184 Warren B. & James Jerome Bell

that *if you draw closer to God, God will draw closer to you.*

The main point to remember about all holy texts is there is always a *lower* and *higher* level of understanding to be had. But in keeping this principle simple, we must all do more than just acknowledge there is a higher power at work. We must in addition to this seek to establish a *personal relationship* with it. God is not something existing *somewhere out there* beyond the clouds and the Sun. To make *contact* with God we only need to *look within.*

So many *believers* are so bull-headed when it comes to their beliefs. And by being bull-headed they invariably *kill the spirit* supporting their testimony. If there is one thing I've learned about information it's that, "No one has a monopoly on knowledge!" Wise

individuals understand that every religious *path*

has something special and unique to add to our

understanding.

This is largely why I do not seek to

religiously adjoin myself to any one particular

path of enlightenment. *There is something I can*

learn from all of them. I never let others cast

their *shadows of doubt* over my openness to

learn new things. *Religious* people often make

you feel *guilty* about not being a *dedicated robot*

in their group or organization.

I remember distinctly a passage in the

Bible where the disciples were complaining to

Jesus about *a different group of believers* who

were in effect *doing the same work* as Jesus and

his crew. The disciples like many religious

members felt that such a Godly work was only reserved for *their group.* To this, Jesus affectionately said: STOP HATING! SO LONG AS *MY FATHER'S WORK* IS BEING DONE IT'S ALL GOOD!

We should not allow ourselves to be controlled by the mentality of *consideration,* which so often causes people to become imprisoned by what other people think and do. Remember, we are only *planters* in God's garden. We do not *own* it! Rather than making the same mistake as Jesus's disciples, I have decided to see myself simply as a member of God's *extended family.* We have no *authority* to appoint the gifts and talents which God gives to his people. As the Bible says, "Every good and perfect gift comes from above." So, who are we to judge?

Although many of us go to the *same*
building every Sunday to worship, I know for a
fact that Jesus did not do this. Jesus was noted
for speaking to the *multitudes (different masses*
of people) whenever he felt God *guided* him to do
so. This is what made Jesus *great.*

Unlike men and their limited level of
understanding, <u>God is not limited!</u> And *Spirit*
can never be contained in any one building or
house. Spirit is *omnipresent.* Jesus once said,
"The Kingdom of God is not a *place* where you
say, lo, it is here or lo, it is there." "The Kingdom
of God is *within* you."

Ultimately, each one of us is a *temple.*
And *church* is wherever a *believer* is at any given
point and time. This of course is not to say that
you should not join a church. But you must

remember that *God's garden* is much larger than *the same square footage of land your church is built on.*

We are no longer in the old dispensation. People no longer need feel they must adjoin themselves to one particular group or sect of *believers.* By staying *open-minded,* I have given myself the opportunity to learn from any path of understanding. I don't need the *building* on the corner of 260ᵗʰ and Euclid to attach myself to as a testament of my faith. I am in *God's presence* whether I worship him by myself or do so among a large group of people.

Honestly, the best way to start on a spiritual path is in a *group.* The key is to make sure the group you join is doing more than just *gathering.* A *gathering* is not the same as an *assembly.* The *body of Christ* does not consist of a *gathering* or *pile* of various body parts. But rather is a proper *assembly* of different body parts aligned to make a *whole.*

But once you reach an *individualized level of anointing,* you no longer need a *man* to teach you what the *anointing within you* can teach you, (1 John 2:27). That is not to say that certain teachers, messengers, or prophets are not needed to bring certain messages to you at certain times. But once you find the *Kingdom of God within you,* you won't need to rely on any *one messenger* to tell you what God can tell you himself.

People always look for *justification* for their stagnant growth. I mean, how can you step outside the *presence* of an *omnipresent God* anyway? How ridiculous. *Either you believe that God is everywhere always or you don't.* Either you are *connected* to God or you are not. Being in a *group* could only mean you are *connected to a group* and not to God. Think about it. If you are a *leg* on the Body of Christ, you cannot help being a *part of the Assembly* of the body of Christ. This fact is irrefutable.

There is a scripture in the Bible which says, "The wisdom of man is *foolishness* with God." And that scripture applies to every bishop, pastor, deacon, prophet, and evangelist you could think of. Unlike many *sheep* still looking for a *shepherd*, I am not *impressed* with the wisdom of any man.

The wisest man on earth is the one who understands that all of his knowledge is but a *farthing* in the sight of God. And if he has any

wisdom to speak of he knows that his wisdom

comes from God. Just because you can *quote*

the Bible or Quran doesn't mean you *practice*

what you preach. Remember, *knowledge does*

not become wisdom until you apply it!

All wise men and women *know* the more

they learn the more they realize what they *don't*

know. All this *holy name calling* and *title bearing*

in the church is a *waste* of time and energy. If I

must address you by a specific *title* or *name* I

would much rather not address you at all!

The church today would be in serious

trouble if Jesus did return. For starters, too

many of the "Saints" are living *double* lives.

There is simply too much homosexuality in the

church for it to be a place of holistic spirituality.

They'll let *anything* and *everything* go on in the church nowadays. And the main reason pastors are reluctant to *keep it real with the people* is because *they don't want to lose their congregations.* I know some of you may disagree with me. But so what?

The path of enlightenment is not for the light-hearted. You cannot be a *spiritual leader* unless you are *following the path* you preach about. Either tell the people the *whole truth* or sit your ass down somewhere.

The road to spirituality begins with *being true to yourself.* This is a deep level of resolve we must all come to grips with. If you are *sincerely right,* you should never be afraid to carry a cross or *two*; if that's what your *faith* requires you to do. Amen.

WITHOUT A VISION...

The purpose of this book is to give its readers the key to *greatness*. Greatness cannot be achieved through the accumulation of money. Although Paula Yates was a successful British TV host, she never achieved *greatness*. Greatness also cannot be achieved by becoming world famous. Robert Pastorelli was as well connected as any person you could think of; but because Robert lacked this *key*, he failed to become *great*.

Greatness can only be attained by understanding the scripture *John 10:14*. "Jesus answered them, Is it not written in your law, I said, *Ye are gods?*" People who lack this understanding will probably believe it is blasphemous to suggest that a man can become *a god.* At no time in Jesus's life did he say he was here to do the will of himself. What made Jesus *a god* was that he understood the key to greatness is *obedience (Luke 22:42).*

Any man or woman can become *great.* The key is to learn how to submit your will to the will of the *Father.* Then, when you speak, it will be the *Father* speaking through you. When you achieve, it will be the *Father* achieving through you. Man will always come up short in his own understanding. But if he will only learn how to *listen* to the *still small voice* of God within him, he will become *great.*

God speaks to *His children* in all important matters of their lives. He cares as much about your finances as He does with the development of your soul. Since *God exists within everything he created,* there is nothing that concerns you that does not concern God.

So often I hear people talk about the importance of good investing. It's true; a *good* investor is light years ahead of an *average* investor. But the question I often ask myself is how many people understand what *good investing* is?

Whenever I'm in a gas station, I always see people lining up to play their *numbers.* For many people, the Lottery is the best way they know to *hedge* their finances. But the Lottery is a crapshoot. And in most cases, so is playing the stock market. In truth, the only people who are doing well in the stock market are the people *selling stocks*. The reason is because the sellers of stock make their money whether the stock goes up or down.

In the stock market, the participants are playing with *dice* known as *capital gains*. This means they *buy a stock* at a certain price in the hopes of *selling it* later for a profit. If there is any gains (profit) made from the investment, the gains are subject to a *tax* known as the *capital gains tax*. Under capital gains, *20 percent of the profit* is owed in taxes. Although, most Americans would like to play the stock market, most don't understand that *betting* on capital gains is about as risky as a *crapshoot*.

Millions of people over the last 10 years bought homes because their real estate broker (salesman) *sold them* on the dream that their home was going to go up in value. But what the broker did not tell them was that he doesn't have a *crystal ball.* This last real estate and stock market crisis has proven one thing. The reason stockbrokers and real estate brokers are called *brokers* is because their financial intelligence is *bankrupt. They don't know what is going to happen* and have *no control* over what happens. My only question is *why are we still listening to these people?*

One reason it is so easy to *fool* the average American on bum deals like this is because they have no *financial intelligence.* As I said once before in this book, *rich people learn about money at home.* They know the school system does not teach the game of money. So, for rich kids to have a decided edge, their parents equip them with financial knowledge they can use as *leverage* over the rest of the *sheep*.

Without a real understanding of money, people become slaves to it. *Sheep* place too much emphasis on money as a goal. This one-sided focus often blinds them to the *fundamental reality* that most rich people understand. That reality is, *money is not real!*

Most people living and working in America are nothing more than *paycheck crack heads.* That is, they are always *fiending for their next fix (paycheck).* In fact, this insatiable need for *the next payday* is the only thing that helps most Americans get through their workweek. "Thank God It's Friday!"

This phrase is not something anyone who *loves their job* would ever say. Many people believe that most popular rap artists have *sold their souls* for money. But what about the fact that most Americans have agreed to exchange their most precious commodity—time—for a paycheck? And when you add the fact that most Americans are *working a job they can't stand,* I'd say rap artists are not the only people who have sold their souls.

Any situation can be handled correctly once it is understood. By first understanding that *money is not real,* you will be better able to assess what you should be *exchanging your time* for. And once you learn to value your *time* more than you value *money,* you can successfully go about the task of *putting money to work for you.* But as long as you give money more credit than it deserves, you will greatly relinquish your ability to *attract it* in large amounts.

Now, just because I said that money is not real does not mean that it is not important. You got to have money and knowledge to help create a better life for yourself. That is why knowing how to keep everything in its proper perspective is so important. Keeping a proper perspective keeps you from overextending yourself on a *pipe dream.* If more people understood money and the way the game of money is played they could play it, too. But as long as your only hope for elevating your lifestyle is winning the lottery, you will probably be in for a rude awakening.

True investing is not a crapshoot. It is based on *careful planning.* The word *vision* as defined by Merriam Webster (online) is: "A thought, concept, or object formed by the imagination." People who understand investing do so in accordance to a *plan*. The plan they use to base their investments upon is based on a *grand vision* of the future. In other words they have a specific *thought* or *concept* about where their investments will take them.

Most people who claim to be investing are really just praying for a miracle to happen. They don't have a definite aim to reach for. And that is precisely why they *never* reach it. *You have to have a vision if you plan to be successful. You have to know where you are going before you invest.*

Men who expect to be leaders must begin their quest with a specific goal in mind. Black men must learn to use *vision* as a way to build

up their self-esteem. It doesn't matter the *way*
people see you. The only thing that matters is
the *way you see yourself.* Using your *vision* of
the future as your greatest source of *motivation*
will give you the confidence to do what you've
never done before. You can't help but *grow in
confidence* when you hold a magnificent image of
yourself in your mind's eye. As long as you can
hold that powerful image in your consciousness,
no one will be able to take it away from you!

A good saying to remember is: "There's no
revenge like success." But what most people fail
to realize is that they don't have to *wait* until
they achieve their goals to be successful.
Success as well as failure is a *decision* that you
make. Whatever the world thinks about me
doesn't matter. *I have already decided to be
successful!* There is *no room* in my

consciousness for negativity. And this is by far the most liberating achievement you will ever realize.

It is the achievement of gaining full control over your *thoughts, moods, and feelings.* Just be a success!!! And remember, having a worthy ideal can only bless you when you learn to protect it. What's the point of throwing *uncovered seeds* on the ground if the *birds* are just going to come and eat them? People who have worthy ideals must learn to *protect them* until they manifest. You have to be *selective* about who you *share* your dreams with.

Most people are nothing more than *birds.* That is, they're out to *take* what is rightfully yours. You can't just go through life thinking *positive* all the time. Sometimes, the only way to protect what is precious to you is to learn to think about the *negative*. At times, you may even have to *threaten* what threatens you.

Life is a consortium of various *seasons* and you've got to know what *actions* are best suited for those seasons. In the *winters* of your life you've got to work more on *yourself* than anything else. The winters of life represent the *slow periods* of business and commerce. You may even have *winters* or slow periods of activity in your social life. The best actions to take in these slow periods are to *add* to your knowledge and understanding. We must all make better use of our winters. Read the books that will make you a better businessperson or social magnet.

You must also listen to lectures that encourage you to *plant new seeds* in the *springs* of your life. Don't just sit on your hands and *wait* for winter to go away. This is the *time* to make *you* better. In the *springs* of life there is *opportunity*. The first action you must take when opportunity presents itself is to *take advantage* of it. If most of your opportunities come in the *spring*, why would you *wait* until the *following spring* to take action? Spring requires you to act now. *You can either plant in the spring or beg in the fall!* The choice is yours.

Summer is a time to *nourish* what is good and *threaten* whatever threatens you. Summer is a time of great activity. It is a time to deal with the *positives* and *negatives* of life. In the *summer* you must always be ready to *love*

206 Warren B. & James Jerome Bell

whatever loves you and *hate* whatever hates you. This is a time for both *offense* and *defense*.

The *fall* is a time of *harvest*. In these times you must *learn to reap without complaint.* *Why would you complain about having no crops to harvest, when you know you wasted your opportunities to plant in the spring?* Over the years, I have heard brothers say: "I'm taking my beating like a man." Real men never complain about the circumstances *they* created.

And you should never *apologize* if you reap little in the fall. As the Bible says in Galatians 6:7, "Do not be deceived: God is not mocked." "Whatsoever a man soweth, that shall he also reap." *No man or woman will ever reach full maturity until they accept full responsibility for their actions.* As I said before: "Five years from now, your income will be the average of your five best friends." So if your five best friends are all broke, you will probably be broke too! You are who you hangout with!

Dr. Martin Luther King Jr. once said: "An oppressed people cannot be oppressed forever." The key to understanding this point is that *freedom can only be achieved once you learn to free yourself.* People who are *waiting for their oppressors* to have a change of heart will undoubtedly wait forever.

The white man will never *free* black people from oppression. To do so would mean he would have to give up all of his *privileges.* To understand anything holistically you must *study it.* When did the white man ever *share* something that he *took* from someone else? Did

208 Warren B. & James Jerome Bell

he share the benefits that came with this land
after he *stole it* from the Native Americans? Did
he show any signs of *humanity* when he killed
off damn near 60 million of these people? And
what *humanity* does he show every opening
season in Cleveland, Ohio when the mascot for
the Cleveland Indians is a big grinning ass
Native American?

What's so funny about your ancestors
being subjected to a devil who commits all out
genocide against them? This is humor only a
devil can find entertaining!!! You are *insane,* if
after all that history, *you still think you can*
change the spots on a leopard. At some point
you will have to *decide* what side of the *slave*
fence you are going to be on. Harriett Tubman
decided she wasn't going to be on the *inside* of

the slave fence. God did not create black people to be anybody's slave!

If freedom is your *goal* then use your desire to be free to *imagine* what freedom looks like for you. Black people need to read up on Daniel 7:25. It talks about the *number of years of our enslavement* in the Americas.

The Creator has been watching our plight brothers and sisters. And He has been keeping strict accounts, being that He is the accountant of all accountants. So, I'm asking you – what *season* is it? Just like a worker who has given a job 20 to 30 years of his life before he retires, how many more years will you work to build somebody else's kingdom?

For the last 400 years, we have worked tirelessly to help massa accomplish *his vision.* I say the *season* has come for us to start

accomplishing ours!

MACHINES

"Then I heard another voice calling from Heaven, Come out of her, my people. Do not take part in her sins, or you will be punished with her" (Revelations 18:4).

We are living in an important *time* in history. It is a *time* where one thing must *fall* so another can *rise* and *takeover*. During the "Age of Pisces," black people took a *short intermission* from power. During that *intermission,* people who now refer to themselves as *white* have done

all maner of evil to God's children.

As I look at the morbid photographs of my

ancestors dangling from a tree, I question

whether the *smiling white faces* underneath

them had a *soul*. Of course, everything in

existence has a *spirit*. Even those objects we

perceive to be *solids* on the material plane. The

fact is *all solids are in motion;* only, the *molecules*

that make them up are *moving so slowly* that

the human eye can't perceive it. This *motion,*

whether perceived or not is called *spirit*.

But *spirit* and *soul* are two *different* things.

To have a *soul* means to be *guided* or *lead* by

that essence. This *essence* is none other than

the microcosm of *God* or *love* in man. All those

who are *guided by love* have a soul. And all

those who are not, <u>don't.</u> What good is it to *have*
something that you never *make use of?*

There is a *spiritual law* that speaks to this.
It's called "The Law of Use." This law says: "If
you do not <u>use</u> what you have, you will <u>lose</u> it."
The soul essence in man falls under the same
law. In the book of Genesis, it says that God
breathed the *breath of life* into man. What this
means is that once the human body is *formed,* it
needs a *spirit* or *breath of life* to become *living* or
animated.

Once the body receives this *breath,* the
Bible says that man *became* a *living soul.* The
thing we must understand is that even though
man is born with a soul essence, it does not
mean that this soul is already *fully developed.*

If you examine a gas stove, you will find there is a *small flame* burning under its top. This *small fire* is known as a *pilot light.* To ignite one of the *eyes* on the stove, the pilot light must already be *lit.* If this pilot light ever *goes out,* you will be unable to *use* the stove.

In much the same way, when man is born, he too has a *small flame* burning inside of him. Science has already *proven* this. Both animals and man breathe in *oxygen* but breathe out *carbon dioxide.*

Whenever a fire is *burning,* it gives off the gas *carbon dioxide.* Therefore, all living humans have this *inner fire.* The only reason the *fire in man* does not consume his body is because it is the *white part* of the flame. The *white* part of a flame is of an *ethereal essence* and does not *consume* material matter.

This is why in certain *eastern cultures,* whenever a loved one dies, the mourners cover themselves in *white ash.* The white ash represents what is *left* after the *fire in man* dies.

But just like the pilot light on a stove, man's *inner flame* only represents his *potential* to *raise his level of consciousness and being.* So, when the Bible says that man <u>became</u> a living soul, it means he was born with the <u>potential to</u> <u>become</u> lead or guided by this essence. The more a man is lead by "The Burning Bush" within him, the greater his inner flame becomes.

According to the scriptures, Jesus the *Christ* had evolved into a *full-fledged flame.* In fact, one reason the image of Jesus is often depicted with a *ray of light surrounding his head* is because he had a *fully developed soul.*

In other words, his light was not a light that *shined on him.* It was a light that *shined in him.* You must remember the word Christ is a *title*, not a *name.* The word *Christ* or *KRST* means *one whose head is anointed with oil.* This *anointing* can only be acquired by learning to submit the will of the *ego* to the will of the *Father.* Such a *submission* can only be mastered *over time.*

People often assume they automatically have a *fully developed soul.* But just like the human body, man's soul must also *mature* and *grow* in him. The soul starts out *small* and can only be *developed* as a result of the *inner struggle within man.* This *struggle* is a battle between the good and evil within man.

To illustrate this fact, I take you to Romans 7:21. It says: "I find then a law that when I would do *good, evil* is present with me." This scripture clearly shows us there is always a *battle* of good and evil brewing within us. It is a battle between the *human personality* and the *soul.* For man to win this *war*, he must first accept that it exists. Otherwise, he will continue to be a *personality* or *mask* without a *soul.*

When the Bible warns us to "Come out of her," it is referring to those of us who live in *Amerikkka.* This scripture is *warning* God's people to resist the urge of the *personality* to follow the patterns of the *virgin daughter of Babylon (Isaiah 47:1).*

218 Warren B. & James Jerome Bell

The main goal of the *personality* is to serve
itself and be *accepted* in society. This need for
acceptance causes people to *go along in order to
get along.* So much of what is thought to be
acceptable behavior in Amerikkka is 100 percent
against God's will. Unfortunately, many *black*
men and women have traded in their *divineness*
for *acceptance* into white America. And as a
result, they have procured the same *fate*
awaiting their oppressors.

"Do not copy the behavior and customs of
this world, but let God transform you into a new
person by changing the way you think. Then you
will learn to know God's will for you, which is
good and *pleasing* and *perfect*" (Romans 12:2).

Even if you are a self-hating black person,
you could not possibly think God is *pleased* with

Amerikkka. In this country, everything that is *good* and *pleasing* to God has been *mixed in* with man's perverseness.

So much of what this country *approves of* is a total debauchery of higher spiritual laws. Even the so called *Christian church* is guilty of destroying God's laws. "Think not that I am come to destroy the law, or the prophets; I am not come to destroy, but to fulfill" (Matthew 5:17).

Many Christian churches today preach the doctrine of *saving souls*. This belief requires them to motivate all *non-believers* into accepting Jesus *Christ* as their personal savior. This belief hinges on the notion that once you say, *I accept Jesus as my personal savior;* your soul is *redeemed* and all your sins are forgiven.

The problem with this doctrine is that it leads *believers* into assuming that *Jesus already paid the price for the development of their souls.* Therefore, all they need to do to acquire salvation and forgiveness is *ask God to forgive them* each time they *fall short* of what is *good,* and *pleasing,* and *perfect* to God. Like the Arm & Hammer "Magic Eraser," the process of soul development will just be *magically wiped away.*

But this is a total misunderstanding of the true *process of salvation.* In truth, man is in no position to *save* another person's soul. In fact, he better make *sure* his own soul has been *saved.* The responsibility of a man's soul rests solely with him.

For instance, if you get pulled over by the police for speeding, Jesus is not going to *pay* your speeding ticket. Neither is the *Holy Spirit*

or the *Father* for that matter.

In the same way, it is erroneous to think

that *Jesus paid the price for your salvation.*

When Jesus died on the cross, he was displaying

his level of commitment to the Father's will. You

are both *ignorant and lazy* if you think you are

excused from needing to do the same. Jesus

carried *his* cross. Now it's time you carried

yours.

Your soul cannot be *saved* by an

emotionally charged *prayer* of faith. It can only

be redeemed as a *testament* of your *life* and

growth over time. The only way a man can save

his soul is to battle for *complete control* over his

lower nature. In other words, man, like Jesus

must *die to the predominance of his personality.*

Remember, they didn't hang Jesus' *soul* on the cross—they hung his *body*. In other words, Jesus sacrificed the will of his *personality* for the will of the Father (Luke 22:42).

In the same way the human body is born *small* and *matures over time,* the soul of man must also follow this same *process. No one is born with a fully developed soul.* But, history has proven there have been and are a few *mothers* who were fortunate enough to birth a child who *attracted* a more *advanced* soul.

When this happens, it is no *accident.* But is the result of a mother who *did certain things during her pregnancy* to cause her baby to *attract a soul* with an advanced level of consciousness. According to the scriptures,

Mary, the mother of Jesus, was one such mother.

According to the scriptures, when Jesus was only *twelve*; he was hanging out and philosophizing with the wisest of men. This was because he was born with a soul that already contained a greater level of *wisdom* than his physical age. "And Jesus grew in wisdom and stature, and in favor with God and man" (Luke 2:52).

Any mothers who are interested in creating *great* children must *study to show themselves approved.* There are plenty of books and much information available to parents on this subject. But for the sake of time, I will leave such studies up to you. The point is the *soul* must be *developed.* And unless man *grows in wisdom and in stature,* he will run the risk of harboring an *undeveloped soul.*

Although you may not have the *insight* to *see* whether a man is a *child of God* -- you can, however, examine his *ways.* When the European was lynching and enslaving black people on a wholesale level, he did so because he <u>thought</u> he was doing the will of God. When the Jews *rewrote* the *Torah* and created the *Talmud*, they told the world *they* were the *chosen of God.* Nobody ever stopped to consider whether their *Talmudic lie* about Black people being the *cursed race of Ham* was true.

Jewish rabbinical scholars lied saying that Noah's son *Ham (a black man) mocked his father in his nakedness.* Jews did not bother to tell you that it would be *impossible* for *any man* to *avoid* seeing his pissy drunk father prancing around in his nakedness. Remember, Ham went so far as to *warn his brothers not to look in their father's room* when they passed by it. Does that sound like a man who found it *amusing* to find his father in such a condition? I suppose if Ham were _white,_ everyone would recognize his *warning* as a testament to his *humanity.*

But this *misinterpretation* did not exist in the Torah*; the original book of the Hebrews.* And please keep in mind the original Hebrew were *all black.* The *white Jews* did not come along until over *1000 years later.* But somehow, this *lie* became a part of the *new doctrine* once the *European* adopted the *Hebrew* faith. How convenient!

"I know your afflictions and your poverty –
yet you are rich! I know about the *slander* of
those who say they are *Jews* and are not, but
are a *synagogue* of Satan" (Revelations 2:9). We
know this is talking about the *modern day Jew*
because a synagogue is defined as: "*A Jewish
house of worship*, often having facilities for
religious instruction."

Remember, the *original* people of this faith
did not refer to themselves as <u>Jews</u>. They called
themselves <u>Hebrews</u> as far back as *1700 B.C.*
And let's not forget, <u>Europe wasn't established
until *1000 B.C.*</u> Therefore, the word *Jew* couldn't
exist until *over 1000 years after* the uneducated
Hebrews entered Afrika from Ur of Chaldea.

The point is, just because someone lies
and tells you that *black people are cursed*, still

doesn't make it *holy* for you to hang them from trees. And as we'll learn later in this chapter, anyone with a *developing soul* already has a sense of what is *good, pleasing* and *perfect* in the sight of God. And killing black people doesn't fall under that category.

The purpose of this book is to give its readers the key to *greatness*. Greatness cannot be achieved through the accumulation of money. Although Steve Clarke had achieved success with Def Leppard, he never achieved *greatness*. Greatness also cannot be achieved by becoming world famous. Herb Abrams was as well connected as any person you could think of; but because Herb lacked this *key*, he failed to become *great*.

Greatness can only be attained by understanding the scripture *John 10:14.* "Jesus answered them, Is it not written in your law, I said, *Ye are gods?*" People who lack this understanding will probably believe it is blasphemous to suggest that a man can become *a god.* At no time in Jesus's life did he say he was here to do the will of himself. What made Jesus *a god* was that he understood the key to greatness is *obedience (Luke 22:42).*

Any man or woman can become *great.* The key is to learn how to submit your will to the will of the *Father.* Then, when you speak, it will be the *Father* speaking through you. When you achieve, it will be the *Father* achieving through you. Man will always come up short in his own understanding. But if he will only learn

how to *listen* to the *still small voice* of God within him, he will become *great*.

One reason it is so difficult for black people in Amerikkka to establish *greatness* is because *evil is always present.* Everywhere you look, you see a world full of *satanic* activity. Just get in your car and take a *drive* for about fifteen minutes. As you drive along, consciously observe the *energy* inherent in the *eyes* of everyone you pass.

You will find that most people contain an *icy energy* in their eyes. In other words, their eyes lack the *warmth* of a true human being. If "The eyes are the *windows* to the soul," then most people living in Amerikkka have an *undeveloped soul.*

People are so *evil* these days that they'll
give you a *dirty look* just for *speaking* to them.
This *icy energy* so often displayed by
Amerikkkans is proof that most westerners lack
true spirituality. If someone has a *developing*
soul, it will prove itself in the way they *relate* to
others. As I said before, the actions of man are
governed by *spirit,* not by *mind.*

The greatest *proof* that certain people lack
a *dominant soul essence* is their collective
inability to *see God in everything that exists.* If
God is <u>omnipresent</u>, then His *spirit* remains
within <u>everything</u> He created. When the world
rulers sit down at *the round table* to discuss new
methods of genocide, they are also discussing
new tactics to *kill the spirit of God.*

But when a man's soul is his *pilot,* he sees the *spirit of God* in everything God created. This *understanding* also won't allow him to stunt or subjugate another man's growth. On the *competitive path,* man sees the world through the eyes of *limitation.* People on this *low level of vibration* view killing *a necessary evil.* That is because they view the world as only having a *limited supply* of natural resources.

God's children on the other hand, follow the *creative path.* On the *creative path,* humans see the world through the eyes of *unlimited potential and possibility.* It is what Deepak Chopra refers to as *pure potentiality.* On the *creative path,* there is *more than enough* to go around. On the *competitive path,* man is in a *mad scramble to get his* before it runs out.

232 Warren B. & James Jerome Bell

In truth, it is not white people who *hate* black people. *It is the spirit of fear working in them that causes them to hate us!* "For our struggle is not against *flesh and blood,* but against the *rulers,* against the *authorities,* against the *powers of this dark world* and against the *spiritual forces of evil in the heavenly realms*" (Ephesians 6:12). As I said, the actions of all men are governed by *spirit,* not by *mind.*

The first buyer of Afrikan slaves were *Christians.* Among the first *buyers* was *Pope Martin the 5th.* Of all people, you would think the Pope would know better. But when you are a *machine,* not even a *title* like Pope can keep you from doing Satan's *wet work.*

If the Pope had a *soul,* his soul wouldn't even allow him to entertain *the buying and selling of black people.* Unless there is an *ongoing struggle* between *right* and *wrong* within a man, *his soul essence* will remain *dormant.*

The longer a man *ignores the voice of God* within him, the *less and less* he will hear it. And over time, both he and his *posterity* will be given over to an *unacceptable mind.* "And even as they did not like to retain God in their knowledge, God gave them over to a *corrupt (unacceptable) mind,* to do those things which are not convenient" (Romans 1:28).

Now before you *cast your stone,* please take the time to look up the word *devil* in a dictionary. One definition defines *devil* as: "An atrociously wicked, cruel, or ill-tempered *person.*" Therefore, *a devil* is not just a *spirit.* It can also be a *man* or *woman.*

In the west, *psychology* is erroneously thought to be *the science of mind behavior.* But in reality, *the actions of man are the physical manifestation of spirit.* This is the reason western medicine is so far off the mark. Since the western man has a *limited spiritual understanding and capacity,* he often tries to solve *spiritual* matters with *physical* antidotes. This is at the apex of western medicine.

All men are governed by a spiritual essence. One spiritual essence desires that all men be *edified, empowered, and transformed by the renewing of their mind.* The other spiritual essence desires to *steal, kill, and destroy everything associated with the original essence.* The phenomena taking place on the *earthly plane* are an exact *replica* of the dramas being worked out on the *spiritual plane.* "Thy kingdom come. Thy will be done in *earth* as it is in *heaven*" (Matthew 6:10).

For Satan to best complete his will through man, he must first have a wide array of *machines* at his disposal. The more a man learns to *think independently,* the harder it is to *control* him.

Most Americans assume they *cause* things to happen in their lives. But usually, people are only *caused* to make things happen. The reason for this is that most men are *too lazy* to govern their *thoughts, moods, and feelings.* Therefore, they remain *robots* awaiting their next *command.*

Among the most repeated *commands* for machines in Amerikkka is *prejudice.* When most Americans see a Muslim Arab wearing a *turban,* their mechanical programming *causes* them to suspect *terrorism.* These same *robots* are also *programmed* to assume that many young black men are *gangster affiliated.* Yet, none of these *machines* ever stop to consider the atrocities caused by their *gangster government.* Talk about a double standard.

<u>When you hate someone you don't even know, you hate them because you are a machine.</u> You hate them because you are *powerless to do* otherwise. All *automations* are governed by *programmed responses.* And no programmed response is a quality of *human intelligence.*

God's children must be ever mindful of the kinds of *spiritual influences* they encounter on a day-to-day basis. *Just because someone appears to be human does not mean they are human.* This same principle applies to those working in religious ministries.

"Not everyone who says, *Lord, Lord* shall enter into the Kingdom of Heaven" (Matthew 7:21). Just because your priest wears a *Godly robe* does not mean he is not a *programmed homosexual pedophile.* That is precisely why God's children must learn to *perceive the spirit* of a man more than the quality of his *personality.*

God has given his children the ability to perceive beyond the *natural.* This *insight* is what is meant as your *third eye.* Remember, most of the people you meet are *machines. And all machines will do you in without a second thought.*

Most Americans are working at a job they can't stand. These automatons have traded in their potential to become *great* in exchange for a *paycheck*. In many intellectual circles, such an action is often referred to as *selling your soul.*

There is a *purpose* for man that is much more profound than *getting his bills paid*. But when that purpose goes *unfulfilled*, man becomes nothing but an *angry machine*. <u>White people who hate black people are only projecting the hatred they feel for themselves.</u> You cannot *give* someone something you do not already have in your *possession*.

Basic psychology tells us the world is only a *mirror* of you. If you hate *yourself*, no *mirror* you stand in front of is going to be your friend. Whenever a certain group of people *poison* the same water supply they must drink from, they are suffering from *self-hatred*. Whenever a certain group of people *pollute* the same air they breathe, they are suffering from *self-hatred.* Whenever certain groups of people *destroy* the same rain forests that help to sustain their existence, they are suffering from *self-hatred.* And whenever a certain group of people *deplete the ozone layer* on the same planet they have to live on, they are suffering from *self-hatred.* No race of people who hates themselves can love anyone on a conscious level. This fact is irrefutable.

No **human being** ever wants a thing until he wants for his *neighbor* what he wants for himself. Black people living in the hells of North Amerikkka must accept the fact that their country is being governed by Satan and his children. Any human being trying to get *machines* to love him is wasting his time. *It is impossible for a machine to produce human love.*

But there is a bright side to all of this. God in his infinite *mercy* is giving man the opportunity to *separate himself from the customs and patterns of this world.*

Judgment is quickly approaching. And only those who *repent* of their sins and *change* their evil ways will escape what is coming. "If *My people* who are called by *My name* will humble themselves, and pray and seek *My face* and turn from their wicked ways, then will I hear from heaven and will forgive their sins and heal their land" (2 Chronicles 7:14).

Far too many black people have compromised their *spiritual integrity* for *acceptance* into this evil society. Black people have adopted alcoholism, homosexuality, lesbianism, and even genocide against *all* indigenous people of the earth. And now it is time to answer for your sins.

Never mind the riches the wicked possess. "A good person leaves an inheritance for their children's children, but a *sinner's wealth* is stored up for the righteous" (Proverbs 13:22).

God's people do not have to enter into a Godless scramble to gain material possessions. That is what Satan requires of *his people.* But we are *above* Satan. "The Science of Greatness" requires us to learn to *create* what we want rather than to *compete* for it. No Child of God has to *compete* with anyone. If he wants something, all he has to do is ask his Father.

"Fear not little flock, for it is your Father's pleasure to give you the Kingdom" (Luke 12:32).

Fear is a spiritual essence that is *opposite* of God. To *fear* is to have the ability to recognize *perceived danger* leading to an urge to confront it or flee from it. Every act of violence ever bestowed on black people by white people was caused by *fear*.

It is fear that creates privilege. But the only way a *privilege* can exist is if there is some form of *subjugation.* It is Satan who gives *privilege* to his children. *But it is God who gives favor to his.* "May the favor of the Lord our God rest on us; establish the work of our hands for us – yes, establish the work of our hands" (Psalms 90:17).

Some *machines* will try to deduce the writings in this book to *reverse racism.* But let me remind you that to *reverse* something means to *move, act, or organize in a manner contrary to the usual.* And in Amerikkka, acting against the progress of black people is the *usual.* A man's *soul* is in jeopardy if he has spiritual knowledge and doesn't make *use* of it.

"But the one who does not know and does things deserving punishment will be beaten with few blows. From everyone who has been given much, much will be demanded; and from the one who has been entrusted with much, much more will be asked" (Luke 12:48).

Everyone is born a machine, be it intellectual, emotional, or physical. Only once you embraces higher consciousness can you have the *potential* to become a human being.

WHITE HISTORY MONTH

The main purpose of this book is to give
its readers the key to *greatness*. Greatness
cannot be achieved through the accumulation of
money. Although Nick Adams was an Academy
Award nominated American film and television
actor, Adams never achieved *greatness*.
Greatness also cannot be achieved by becoming
world famous. Kerry Gene Adkisson was as well
connected as any person you could think of; but
because Kerry lacked this *key*, he failed to
become *great*.

245   **Warren B. & James Jerome Bell**

Greatness can only be attained by
understanding the scripture *John 10:14.* "Jesus
answered them, Is it not written in your law, I
said, *Ye are gods?*" People who lack this
understanding will probably believe it is
blasphemous to suggest that a man can become
a god. At no time in Jesus's life did he say he
was here to do the will of himself. What made
Jesus *a god* was that he understood the key to
greatness is *obedience (Luke 22:42).*

Any man or woman can become *great.*
The key is to learn how to submit your will to
the will of the *Father.* Then, when you speak, it
will be the *Father* speaking through you. When
you achieve, it will be the *Father* achieving
through you. Man will always come up short in
his own understanding. But if he will only learn

how to *listen* to the *still small voice* of God within him, he will undoubtedly become *great*.

With that said, there is one *great* characteristic I would now like to discuss. It is the subject of charisma. In the words of my partner James, charisma is: "The manifestation of a God-like presence within an individual that permeates outwardly." In the dictionary it reads that charisma is: "A rare quality attributed to leaders who arouse fervent popular devotion and enthusiasm."

While parlaying in a black owned fragrance shop, I had the opportunity of meeting Dr. Wade Nobles. Dr. Nobles is a black psychologist and author in Cleveland, Ohio. We were all discussing the subject of *influence* in Amerikkka from *politricks* to leadership. Dr.

Nobles then took a pen and a small piece of paper and wrote on it: "Power is: The ability to define your ideas of reality and to have others believe in those ideas as if they were their very own." After writing down his definition of power, Dr. Nobles then signed it and gave the piece of paper to me.

I felt honored that the good doctor would take such an interest in me to share his knowledge and understanding. Although there are people in our society who have a substantial amount of money, that does not mean they have real *power*. Those individuals who possess real power are the real movers and shakers in the world.

Being that the average person lacks this ability, it holds that most people are looking for powerful personalities to *lead them.* Because of the way most of us were *educated* in Amerikkka, we fail to become *great.* And as you'll learn as the chapter continues, we largely have *white history month* to thank for this.

Because of *white history month,* you would be surprised at the numbers of Americans who do very little *thinking.* In fact, a large number of us are afraid of our own thoughts. These people often keep the television or radio on constantly to keep them *sedated* from the rigors of *thinking.* Because of this, most people in this country *never grow.*

In Amerikkka, one of the key reasons people who read a lot of positive books never *evolve* is because they were not *educated* on how to *sit quietly and think.* You've got to *think* in order to input new information into your

conscious and subconscious mind. Otherwise,

you should just *entertain yourself* with another

positive lecture. People who want real change

must educate themselves on *the art of thinking.*

What's the point of *studying to show*

thyself approved when you implement very little

of what you study? Because of *white history*

month, most Americans don't understand the

power of personal *will.* That is why most people

talk more than they *walk.* If you are a Christian,

I will know it by the way you treat me. Don't

talk me to death. If you are a *living example* of

your faith you won't have to *say* anything. Your

light will say it for you.

Unfortunately, *we live in a white Christian*

society without Christ. For this reason,

countless numbers of God's black male children are incarcerated. Because of *white history month,* the Amerikkkan public accepts the perception most white people have of black men – that is usually *negative.*

But what *white history month fails* to teach its citizens is that only an *animal* would create a *cage* to house another *human being.* If *white history month* in Amerikkka *fails* to educate humans on the true characteristics of *humanity,* it will explain why so few people in the west have a *developing soul.*

People who don't have a *developing soul* feel no remorse when their government gives *syphilis* to Black men in Tuskegee for 40 years. People who don't have a *developing soul* would never admit that in the ancient Afrikan world,

there was no word for *jail* because no one had
ever been to one.

White history month has also miseducated
whites into thinking they are in a *moral position*
to *decide* who is *human* and who is not. *Silly!*
Every man's *humanity* is based on *the way he*
treats his neighbor.

If white people were educated properly in
Amerikkka, they would have *never* tried to
justify the enslavement of blacks. There is no
justification for hanging the original man of the
earth on a tree, cutting off his penis, sticking his
penis in his mouth, and then setting his
mutilated body on fire. Does that sound like
something *Jesus* would do?

White history month is the cause for the
justification of damn near 60 million Native

Americans being slaughtered. The white man would have never survived on this continent without the Native American. But because of *white history month,* he feels no *guilt* when he ruthlessly murders the indigenous people of the world.

White history month was also the *justification* for the raping of countless numbers of *underage black girls* on the white man's so-called plantations. Not to mention the fact that he also is the biggest *deadbeat father* the world has ever known.

The white man is also the most *arrogant* man on earth. But arrogance is not confidence. *Arrogance is overcompensation for all that is lacking.* And it is *arrogance* that keeps white people from *admitting* that both they and the

European Arabs were the principal orchestrators of the Afrikan slave trade.

Christianity came from *Alexandria* in Afrika. *St. Augustine* was a black Christian who wrote books about Christianity in Afrika before the European had given Christianity a second thought. One of the books Augustine wrote was called: "On Christian Doctrines." The fact is the white man's *version* of Christianity was also his *justification* for all the evil he did to non-white people throughout the world. Was not one of the slave ships that transported black people against their will called, *"The Jesus?"*

I write these *facts* not to dwell on the past. But rather to show you that in many cases, *the apple is still hanging on the tree.* No one can judge a man because no man is in a moral position to do so. But, I say these things

because spiritual law says that *man judges*

himself based on the way he acquiesces to God's

laws.

At least *eight times* in the Bible we are

told to *love our neighbor* as we love ourselves.

This is one of the Bible's most repeated

commands. And according to the Bible, your

neighbor is any *stranger* who is in need.

Your *neighbor* is not the people who *look*

like you in your neck of the woods. But rather,

it is *anybody who is near-by where ever you may*

be. Since we are all *neighbors*, tell me with a

straight face that Jesus would have supported

the enslavement of the black man in Amerikkka.

And tell me with a *straight face* that the 100

plus years of continued subjugation of your

black neighbors after slavery would have been deemed as *Christ-like* in Jesus' eyes.

Don't argue with me about the couple of people in your race who openly showed their humanity. They have humanity. I'm talking about the *overwhelming majority of you* who *still* enjoy the *benefits* that come with the subjugation of the black man in Amerikkka. *No black man has to prove his humanity to white people.* They have to *prove* their humanity to us.

One of the reasons black men are constantly incarcerated in this country is because we are the most feared in Amerikkka. It's *too risky* for the white man to allow the black man to have *free rein* to express and profit from the many gifts God has given him. Seeing the black man in all of his glory would undoubtedly cause white Amerikkka to *bow down* to the reigning champion of humanity.

I say *champion* because in spite of all the lies, blood shed, and cover ups in history, the black man still manages to pick himself up and put the many broken pieces of his history back together. *White history month will not succeed at keeping the black race down.* It is *white history month* that would have you believe that black people are *jungle* oriented people. What the *white liars* of history fail to tell you is that *not a single high culture or civilization of Afrika grew up in the jungles.* In fact, *Afrika has less jungle than any other continent comparable to its land mass.* If you don't know this it proves that black history month is not just in *February* -- it is *everyday* of the year.

As I look back at black people's struggles in the 60s, I realize the danger of Dr. King's philosophy. Without knowing it, Dr. King was postulating a philosophy that would quickly annihilate *white genetic material* on the earth. Think about it. What would have happened to the *white race* had they put aside their *prejudices* and freely mixed their genes with melanin based people? *White* would disappear.

Had that happened, Amerikkka would be much *browner* today than any of us could possibly imagine. Therefore, *white genetic survival is incumbent upon prejudice.*

It is in the white man's best interest to keep enmity between him and the black man. In fact, his *genetic survival* depends on it. As the *original* man of the earth, Barack Obama's father still produced a *black man* even though he mixed his genes with those of a white woman. You would not see a mixed child pumping his gas if you saw Barack somewhere and didn't know who he was. You would see what I see – a black man!

As black men with charisma, James and I often try to get black women to see that our reality in Amerikkka is very different from the black woman's. Black women are not a threat to the "Establishment" whether she is feminine or *playing a masculine role* for the time being.

The only thing that matters to the power structure is that black women *play their role* in the destruction of black manhood. <u>Every black sister who participates in this dubious achievement is a **devil**</u>.

I write these things only to serve as a
warning. It is a warning to discard all spiritual,
mental, social, and philosophical alliances you
have with those in power. When your massa
falls dead on his face, you who supported his
rise and ways will fall with him. This *fall* will be
due more so to *group think* than anything else.

In truth, most people are not fit to be
called *individuals.* This lack of *individuality* in
the west is why it is so easy to con the masses. If
you remember, *Herodotus* was named: "The
father of history." But most white educators will
not tell you that Herodotus said *the arts,*
sciences, even the use of speech; the white man
owes to the black man. Why is that?

Is the European's ego so *fragile* that he
must continuously prop-it-up with lie after lie?

The first white Jesus was not painted until 1509 A.D. by Michael Angelo for Pope Julius II. In fact, as early as 1298 **B.C.** in the Temple of Seti 1 in Abydos, you will see the entire story of the Immaculate Conception and virgin birth.

Search the pages of history as well as the *papyri* of ancient Kemet and you'll prove this fact to yourself. Any Afrikan *facts* that would inspire confidence and empowerment in the psyche of black men in Amerikkka are *ignored.* What about the fact that the Afrikan hieroglyphs were already being used by black people two centuries before the establishment of *Egypt* in a place known as *Ta-Seti?* Ta-Seti was among the earliest Nubian Kingdoms that predated Egypt. *Central east Afrikans* didn't need Champollion to be the "Father of Egyptology" before they migrated *up the Nile* into northern Afrika. Silly!

So I humbly ask you, what *month* in the year is *white history month?* I'll tell what *month – **January, March, April, May, June, July, August, September, October, November, and December!*** This is **white history month!!!**

White history month is the reason why the western educational system *fails* to educate white Amerikkka about their Afrikan *mother and father.* *White history month* is also the reason why Amerikkka is *sitting at the back of the bus* in education throughout the world.

White history month is the reason the job market in Amerikkka is so shitty. It is also the reason this country is no longer *in control* of its own money supply. In fact, every third world country is thanking Amerikkka for *white history month* because it has allowed them to advance themselves on to the world stage.

What helped to <u>advance</u> the European's first civilization was *humility*. It was the humility of the Greeks when they first invaded Afrika that allowed them to make themselves *students* of the black masters. It wasn't until the 18th Century when slavery had been put into place that *white history month* was conceived. It was conceived when the European began to doubt those Greek philosophers who told them that the black man and woman was the white man's greatest teachers. Until the European is able to escape his need to *control history*, white history month will hurry the <u>decline of Amerikkka</u> just as it hurried the <u>decline of Rome.</u>

TRUE GENTLEMEN OF LEISURE

Knowledge of self is essential to good communication. No matter how informed you may be you still have to be able to successfully convey that knowledge to others. But like this book, all knowledge must come with a *price.* The wisest of men know that anyone who has an in-depth understanding of a subject should *charge people* for it. The reason is simple; people don't *value* what is *free* as much as they value what they *have to pay for.*

Back in the day there was a group of black poets who called themselves *poor righteous teachers.* Their claim to fame was the fact that even though they were *rich in knowledge,* they still considered themselves as being *poor.* Many black trailblazers of the past like Malcolm X, Dr. Yosef Ben Jochannon, Dr. John Henrick Clarke, Dr. Chancellor Williams, and John G. Jackson are *gods* to the black race.

We would all still be in darkness had not these beacons of light cast their *rays of enlightenment* on our paths. To my elders, I am eternally grateful that I have been blessed to be able to stand on their shoulders – Ashay!

But there is one truth that disturbs me most about the way many of our great black leaders end their lives and careers. Although many of them became successful at *selling black*

people on the truth, most of them still died poor.

There is something to be said about this.

Although, many of our great black teachers have

evolved beyond the levels of *religiosity,* most of

them still see themselves as *unworthy* of riches.

To this day many black people still feel God's

servants are best served *poor* and humble before

the people. It is an idea carried over from old

Christendom.

We all know the dangers inherent in

blazing a new untapped trail. Although there is

great potential for gain, there is also the grave

danger of befalling a fatality. Pioneers are brave

souls. They are willing to take the risks involved

in putting their necks on the line for the good of

the whole. The only problem with this is when

the masses, who lacked the *courage* to be

ostracized, fail in their duty to morally and financially secure their leaders.

That is why anyone who has something of *value* to add to society must understand its *worth*. People who do not mean to be disrespectful often *devalue* what is left in their hands to evaluate. That is precisely why you can't leave the world with the responsibility of properly evaluating what you have to offer. You must determine its *value* yourself.

Knowledge is a privilege. It's a privilege because not everyone is *blessed* to have it. But that is not to say that people who lack this *blessing* can't acquire some semblance of it. The first thing anyone wishing to benefit from knowledge must do is be *open minded* to new information.

At times people fail to be open to new information because they may be jealous of the person bringing it. Many squares fall into this category. Instead of a square learning to feel happy for a player's come-up, *they block their own blessings* by giving in to their feelings of *envy.*

Envy is considered one of the *seven deadly sins* because it causes people to forfeit the spiritual principle of *thankfulness.* Having a *spirit of thankfulness* is a principle and state of mind that will help you to become *one with the universe.* Being one with the universe will put you in a better position to *receive* whatever you ask for on a universal level.

People who wish to live a life of *success* must learn to raise above all negative emotions.

Rather than feeling *jealous* over someone else's good fortune or feeling the need to discredit them for doing well, you need to learn to *feel happy* for them.

Harboring *negative emotions* like jealousy keeps people from getting a *word* that may help them to elevate their circumstances. *The Creator never created the human body to house negative emotions.* Even having feelings of anger should be something that is ephemeral.

You should not carry around feelings of anger for any extended period of time. These negative emotions are *toxic* and can only hinder your spiritual blessings. That is why you will hear me reiterate time and again in this book the importance of *controlling your thoughts, moods, and feelings.* Without such a control, you can be certain to have no power or influence over anything else. All men and women are part man and part animal. The problem with most *men* is that they are largely governed by the *animal* part of them. Whites who have no control over their *thoughts, moods, and feelings* don't understand themselves. They don't realize that their *aggression* towards non-white people is only the outward expression of *animal fear.*

Whenever an animal attacks a man it is because it is afraid on some level. By not analyzing the *impetus* behind your actions, you will invariably become a *slave* to your *lower animal self.* People who have no control over their lower animal natures are not fit to be called *men.* Regardless of your wealth and privilege in Amerikkka, you are a *degenerate human* without total control of your entire being.

For many in this country, the only way they can achieve greatness is to hold somebody else down! The main problem in this is that the *karmic debts* associated with their actions often fall on their posterity. That is precisely why the Bible warns that: *the sins of the Father will fall upon the children even unto the third and fourth generation* (Exodus 34:7.)

Despite this fact this is a very exciting time. We are living in a day that carries two dispositions. On one hand, *the new breed* of players and leaders are beginning to emerge onto the world stage. Many of these future giants have only lived in a world of *computers*. These individuals are young, *fresh,* and much more advanced than the generations that came before them.

In the past it took the average business leader time, energy, adequate support, and a considerable amount of money to successfully launch a new business. But in the *information age*, success may be just a *click* away. In the information age, no one will be able to keep the masses of people ignorant of meaningful information.

The main failure of the Amerikkkan educational system is that it was not formulated to *educate* people. The true mark of education is to teach the student to be a responsible handler of power. But what *power* does the average American citizen have when most of the information they received in school is faulty?

Most of the information we received in school was designed to *sell us* on an elusive

array of concepts.   Concepts like *freedom,*
justice, equality, truth, and self-determination are
nothing more than elaborate fantasies. Just ask
the Native Americans or the Afrikans in
Amerikkka whether these *concepts* hold water.

   If Americans were really educated in this
country, they would know that none of us are free
until everybody is made free. And as long as
politics remain the principal antidote used to
address the ills of our society; *no human animal*
living in the west will ascend to the level of
humanity.

   I think one of the key issues paralyzing
the evolution of the average American is their
blind trust in their government. Nobody wants
to live in a *free society* that lacks freedom for the
general citizenry. In school, we are taught that

hard work is the key success. Although this seems to be an ennobling concept, the real players in life *work smarter* than they ever would hard.

Look at Amerikkka. How can we work hard when there are hardly any jobs? And besides, in this day and age, money is being transferred much faster than in the *good old days.* Rather than you opening up a storefront business with just enough capital to last you for a few months; you need to join the ranks of today's internet moguls. Today's business leaders are exchanging goods and services for cash while having sex in an overseas hotel suite. Simply *waiting* for your next customer to walk in to your establishment is as *primitive* as trying to get ahead by being *competitive.*

In today's new world, ecommerce has greatly leveled the playing field. People who were once thought to be *on the outside* of the game are beginning to see the incredible opportunities available to them. This *coming of age* is shattering the foundations of oppression, usury, and classism.

The internet is by far the greatest threat to the "Establishment." The reason for this is that certain groups have always benefited from the privilege of having *inside information.* It is no mystery that the rich have controlled what we learned in school. The General Education Board, founded in 1903, was created by John D. Rockefeller; its purpose was to *control* what information we received in school.

Why would a *slave owner* teach his slaves knowledge that would enable them to *free themselves* from their slave master? The whole purpose of owning slaves is for those slaves to work hard to fill your pockets. Slave owners are not concerned with creating more *competition* for themselves. They want as much control over their industry as is allowed under the law.

It's often not until people reach their forties that they begin to realize the vicious *cycle* they are in. It is the cycle of go to work, pay the bills, and then go back to work. When such people get a raise or come into a sudden windfall of cash, they often *spend more* to show off their new found wealth.

The end result is a life full of depreciating liabilities with almost zero assets to speak of.

Welcome to the American way! With my in-depth understanding of psychology, I am convinced that there is always a *still small voice* buried inside the consciousness of people. This *voice* is forever trying to hip us to the games being played on a grandeur scale. The problem is most people refuse to *be still* long enough to listen to it.

The main purpose of this book is to give the reader the key to *greatness*. Greatness cannot be achieved through the accumulation of money. Although Michael Brent Adkisson achieved success as a professional wrestler, Michael never achieved *greatness*. Greatness also cannot be achieved by becoming world famous. Dennis Allen was as well connected as any person you could think of. But because

Dennis lacked this *key*, he failed to become *great*.

Greatness can only be attained by understanding the scripture *John 10:14.* "Jesus answered them, Is it not written in your law, I said, *Ye are gods?*" People who lack this understanding will probably believe it is blasphemous to suggest that a man can become *a god.* At no time in Jesus's life did he say he was here to do the will of himself. What made Jesus *a god* was that he understood the key to greatness is *obedience (Luke 22:42).*

Any man or woman can become *great.* The key is to learn how to submit your will to the will of the *Father.* Then, when you speak, it will be the *Father* speaking through you. When you achieve, it will be the *Father* achieving through you. Man will always come up short in his own understanding. But if he will only learn how to *listen* to the *still small voice* of God within him, he will undoubtedly become *great*.

The key to putting yourself in position to receive this *greatness* is to first set up your life in such a way that you will have the *free time* to listen to God's voice. And that's where men like me and James come in. Not to be braggadocios, but James and I are what you would call true "Gentleman of Leisure."

In truth, black men like us are an anomaly to white people. While everyone else is working hard to get ahead, we are probably somewhere in a nail salon getting our nails and feet done. Men of Leisure disdain concepts like:

work hard, pay bills, and give Uncle Sam *half* of all the money you make.

In fact, one of the reasons our society keeps us so bogged-down with daily responsibilities is so we won't have time to relax and come up with solutions to our problems. But for true "Gentlemen of Leisure," our main responsibilities are resting, dressing, and thinking of potential *angles* to make our lives better.

This is probably one of the greatest privileges that can come with being rich. Rich people, who know the game, understand the untapped potential inherent in *uninterrupted thought.* It is through the act of *thinking* that a man can create solutions to his problems. And like I said before, it is only through one's *quiet time* that a man can *hear* from the Father.

While bankers and Wall Street crooks rob businesses and shareholders of billions, James and I use our innate talents for *leisure* to figure out ways to beat the system. It's unfortunate that the only games many black men feel they have left to play are considered *out of bounds* by the greater society.

Like many things that are said to be *outlawed* in Amerikkka, most drugs don't become *illegal* until they get in a black man's hands. The only reason *young white users* are not convicted of drug crimes on a more regular basis are because most police officers are too busy racially profiling black men. For some strange reason, white drug offenses are less likely to make the news headlines.

The main thing *non-human beings* don't understand is that most black people who do illegal shit to get ahead have the *same motivation* as white folks who do the same. Only, there is no *secret* stimulus plan set-up for the sustenance of black wealth like there is for white wealth. Let us not forget that the *average white family* in Amerikkka has 12 times the accumulated net worth of their black counterparts.

Today, even white working class families on average making less than *$15,000* a year (the poverty limit) have the same average net worth as a black family with *$60,000* or better.

Starting in the middle of the 20th century, the U.S. government gave *hundreds of billions* of dollars of equity by way of FH or VA loans to *white people.* These *secret loans* were made to white families to help them procure a little property to sustain *white wealth.* Such loans were all but *off limits to black folks* at this time in history. Sure, any *devil* can search through the pages of history to find some way to *validate* his privilege. But until he comes to grips with the *truth,* he will still be a *devil* none the less.

This is the danger inherent in left brain thinking. The left part of the brain is driven by the process of deductive reasoning. Even when it is obvious that a particular practice or policy is *unfair,* people *polarize* in their left hemisphere a *logical* explanation for it. This also is why these same people will support almost anyone of

their own race even when they know they are
dead wrong.

The fact is that there are a number of
people in our society who are *devoid of soul*
(vampires). They are succubus' who *feed* on the
essence of the *children of light.* It is such
vampires who routinely pull black men over and
have their cars searched for drugs. Meanwhile,
young *white* boys who are *four times as likely* to
have illegal substances on them are able to drive
on by. Sometimes I wonder whether "Travon
Martin" would have still been shot and killed if
he were not wearing a *hoody.*

So what's a player to do? While I do not
condone any form of criminal activity, it would
be *inhumane* of me to knock another man's

hustle. With that said, I will now give you a true

definition of a "Gentleman of Leisure."

> A "Gentleman of Leisure is: ["A
> man who derives a living from his own
> financial assets or has other sources of
> irregular income leaving him
> financially secure without any typical
> employment, duties or financial
> responsibilities. Such a man may be
> self-made, or he may be the result of
> an inheritance, a trust fund baby, or
> an idiot's son. A true gentleman of
> leisure enjoys a high quality of life
> involving mostly recreation and leisure
> activity and often prides himself as a
> playboy, adventurer, or a gentleman
> gambler."] This definition was taken
> from the online Urban Dictionary.

True charisma is something you must be

born with. For people with an overabundance of

this gift, working a regular job is not an option.

There's no better way to upset a true

"Gentleman of Leisure" than to tell him he needs

to get a job. No "G.O.L." worth his salt is going

285 Warren B. & James Jerome Bell

to trade in his *freedom* for a paycheck! That doesn't even sound right.

Players and player partners place their *freedom* above all else. No one will get away with aggressively standing over a "G.O.L." without running the risk of getting his ass kicked. True players are among the few people on earth who qualify to call themselves *individuals*. Most other people are *programmed machines*. Most players have held a lot of jobs in their working careers.

We simply don't take orders well from other people. "G.O.L's." cannot be lead because they were born to lead. But they will take instructions from other players. Usually such instructions come from more established players in the game.

My partner James and I have had at least 40 jobs each throughout our working careers. To most *squares* this would sound like James and I are *unstable.* But to explain it in the simplest way possible, working for *the white man* is not in the *stars* for us.

Whether people know it or not, all of us are all being *controlled by a force* much greater than ourselves. Whenever men try to *force* what is not *natural* on them they often find themselves running into a brick wall.

That is why most players are singled out by many of their superiors on the job. This *singling out process* is not always intentional. In fact, most of what people do is a byproduct of *programmed responses.* That is why Jesus said: "Father forgive them, for *they know not what they do....*" People who do things *without*

thought are not fit to be called human. They are

only fit to be called *machines.*

It is not until a man learns how to *look at*

himself more than he does at others, that he will

be fit to be called *a man.* A man who wishes to

evolve past the *scum* busters in his society must

keep his thoughts and overall focus *at home;*

meaning *on himself.*

People who are of an artistic nature must

find jobs that will give them more room to

express their unique talents. And another thing

about jobs is that you should always choose jobs

for what you will *learn* more than what you will

earn. If you are going to *trade in your time*, it

better be for more than just a paycheck. As long

as you have breath in your lungs you need to be

adding to your knowledge. Taking on a job that you can't stand, but that pays well is abominable! I only hope you learn to *love yourself* more than that.

Speaking of jobs, my business partner James has had various jobs in, real estate, insurance, notary, television and appliance sales, furniture, ladies shoes, and even waiting tables. The main problem James and I have with most employers is that they rarely hire employees to *think*. So, when they come across black men who are not *buck-dancers* they get a little unnerved.

After many failed attempts at developing a successful working relationship with employers, James decided to *sell his services* on his own. At first his businesses were just a way to supplement his irregular income. But being the *sly man* that he is, James always made sure he had a regular *check* coming in every month.

Among the more consistent vehicles James has used in the business world is *consulting*. Since he enjoys helping people solve their problems and accomplish their goals, James has no problem with helping people develop their business plans.

In addition to this, James also *sells* head stones, markers and urns under the umbrella of: "Bell Memorial, LLC." For his business services, James' fees are comparable to what other professionals charge. James has various LLC ventures and as quiet as it is kept, he does all of his own paperwork. He has even done some work for me. He is a *professional.* And the truth is, he is worth much more to his clients than what he is paid.

Despite what Amerikkka may think about black men, I know a lot of brothers like James. You are who you hang out with! Of all of my player friends and associates, I've noticed that we all have a bit of a *sly* nature about us. Of all the people in the world, those individuals who collect most of *your* mortgage payments, credit card payments and taxes are all *sly*? In fact, the cleverest men on earth are those who are in *the top 10 percent* of society. *All these players do all day long is think of new and improved ways to take more money off of you!* So James and I figure, if you can't beat them, *join them.*

Whether people understand our lives or not. As *men of leisure,* it is our duty to create as many elaborate schemes as we can. Such schemes are designed to help us to better supplement our incomes in this dog eat dog white man's world.

In the *early* days of James' life and career, his schemes were much more elaborate and risky. Although I will refrain from further elaboration, the key to remember about all of James' escapades is that at no time did he use his own money.

The main problem with many enterepreneurs is that they rarely understand the important role that *debt* can play in their ventures. Although debt can be very dangerous, *debt can also make you rich if you know what you're doing.* Knowledgeable business people often use *debt* to invest in their businesses. It is what many students of business refer to as:

"O.P.M." (Other People's Money).

The thing you must remember is that in all of James' elaborate schemes, he always made sure he had a definite stream of income coming in every month. This speaks to another key issue I have with many people in business. Most small business owners only raise *just enough* capital to open up their doors and stock their shelves. Then, they rely on the astronomical income that their businesses are supposed to automatically bring in.

As I'm sure you know, most things don't go exactly the way we plan them to. In business, one of the most important skills any entreprenuer can learn is the ability to continually raise money. No one with sense would count on a new business being profitable in it's first year of business. It takes time. The fact is, 9 out of 10 businesses fail within the first 5 years of operation. Nine out of 10! So, you've got to find creative ways to *continually raise money on the side* during your first five years of business.

And these creative ways to continually raise money for your business need to be implemented into your business plan at the outset. Smart business people don't rely on an *unproven business* to immediately be able to support itself.

Since I too am a consultant, I sometimes ask my business clients how they intend to support their businesses if profits don't loom as much as they initially projected them to. If you are openning a new ice cream shop, perhaps you could put an ATM machine inside your store. Although, an ATM machine will not be a major *part* of your overall operation, it will at least provide you with some *on the side income.*

If your ATM machine does well, perhaps you could invest in an additional machine to strategically place in a second location. The point is, these machines will provide you with some *on the side capital* to help you get through the lean years of business.

Again, the goal of implementing *income producing assets* into your busines plan will help you avoid a common mistake made by most entrepreneurs. That mistake lies in the entrepreneurs being the *only real assset* the business *owns.* What if the business owner walks out into the street on a rainy Sunday and gets run over by a Greyhound Bus?

If the entrepreneur is the only *asset* his business *owns*, there will be no more business to speak of if he dies. Entrepreneurs who are smart should plan for every possible contingency. And then, plan a little more. Far too many good ideas have died with their creators. So be smart and don't let that happen to you!

I once heard a saying that says, "All good salepeople are part *con* artist." Well it's true. James once accumulated far too many bad marks on his credit report. So, he went into *con mode* and craftily disputed all of these negative marks. Fortunately for him, his con was orchestrated well enough to have *every negative mark* on his credit rating completely removed.

On another occasion James ran up an excessive number of student loans. And again he had to reach deep into his con bag. The *trick* he pulled out was to tirelessly dispute these *descrepancies* until all of his debts were completely forgiven. Isn't that wonderful?

Many years ago James sent a *fictituous wire* to a money mart inside of a shopping mall. The initial wire was for multiple stacks. But as the cashier attempted to process the wire, she ran into some *issues*. Once again, James used his *mouth piece* and conned the lady into settling for a measely stack. Of course, he *pretended* to be upset at the whole ordeal. But once the store clerk handed him the cash, James made a swift dash for the store exit.

As tough as white folks often make it for Afrikans in this country, there are some advantages to being black. For starters, many whites are too stupid to think that it is even possible for a black man to con them. This often leaves whites *open* for a sneak attack from those *black foxes* who know how most crackers think.

As much as whites create stipulations in their laws to keep black folks out of the mix, black geniuses are always finding new ways to get roses to grow through the concrete. For instance, the Chinese used Sun Tzu to get back at Amerikkka. Instead of attacking a monster from its key points of strength, wise fighters focus on exploiting a monster's *weaknesses.*

Everyone including the Chinese know that Amerikkka's greatest weakness is consumerism. Consumerism is also how the few rulers of this nation keep the masses from rising up in total anarchy. As long as the *machines* are happy, they will never revolt collectively against their government. Pretty ingenious hugh? And since China knows this, they don't mind producing the goods that we want at dirt cheap prices. So long as Americans keep giving foreign countries more money than these countries are giving back to Amerikkka, it will only be a matter of time.

The worst thing you can be in this world is a man who does not take the time to get to know himself. It is difficult to *be true to yourself* when you don't know yourself. *Today, almost everything in most American homes has a "Made in China" sticker on it.* Sun Tzu at its finest!

Taking America off of the gold standard proves that the white man is *clever*. But he is not *wise*. The Founding Fathers of this nation did not want a centralized banking cartel printing America's money. Every President including Nixon knew this. But *greed* caused Nixon in 1971 to push aside his nationalistic commitments to Amerikkka. He struck up a very profitable deal with world bankers and as they say, "The rest is history."

If there's one thing James told me about all of his elaborate schemes, it's that *he enjoyed every minute of it!* Other than for his actions breaking his mother's heart, James has no regrets! Unfortunately, that is more than we can say about the rest of the western world.

Men should live their lives to the fullest. Why do a thing if you're going to be half-stepping? Although James came across a lot of money in his life, he also learned a lot. Now, his game is much more refined.

Like a lot of players, when "J" was a younger man, he didn't care much about consequences. For instance, he once opened up multiple checking accounts at the same time. "J" was spending money like he was a black Donald Trump. To give you an example of his foolish displays of wealth, he once wrote out a check for *$10,000* and gave it to a stripper as tip. Luckily for James, the damsel was too scared to try and cash it.

During the peak of his exploits, James had the pleasure of partying with some of Cleveland's finest babes. Women from different suburbs would come into the city to party with him at places like "The Top of the Town." James was never so selfish that he was unwilling to share in the fruits of his labors. His only requirement was that people know how to have fun and not take themselves too seriously.

If there's one thing James and I can convey about what we have learned thus far in life, it would be to recognize the importance of being *happy*. Any man who has found true happiness *within* himself won't need material possessions or money to make him happy. This is of the most importance.

And another point we would like to make is that *it's not about what you have; it's about how you live!* Anyone can learn to *live well*. We both have a great selection of top designer brands in our wordrobe. But some of our pieces were found in a thrift shop for only a fraction of the actual cost.

Even today, when I shop in a designer store I always look to see what *treasures* I can find buried on the the *clearance rack*. You'd be surprised what deals are lurking there. Remember, expensive taste does not always have to come with an expensive price.

Our experiences have taught James and I that one of the hardest things for any "Gentleman of Leisure" to do is to find a woman who *accepts us* just the way we are. So often

women date a man with their own *agenda* of
what he is supposed to eventually become. But
that is not what true love is all about.

As I said more than once in this book, a
man cannot rise higher than the *quality* of his
woman. But in order for that to happen, a man
must first find a woman who will *accept him*
lock, stock, and barrel. Otherwise, the
relationship will feel more like a long prison
sentence than being truly in-love.

People must understand that true love has
more to do with *sacrifice* than most people
realize. That is why it is so important that
women take the time to *know who they are*
choosing before they choose. Anyone can
successfully *sell themselves* and thereby attract
a quality mate. But like money, it's not about

how much love you make. It's about *how much love you keep!* Spoken from true "Gentlemen of Leisure." Peace!!

MONEY AIN'T A THANG!

If those in power had a philosophy it would be: <u>Why make understanding money *simple* when you can make it *hard.*</u> Most people fear discussing the topic of money. I guess they have *white history month* to thank for this. You would be surprised how many people *$ell their souls* for something they don't understand.

Just look at all the people who work at jobs they don't like. These people are exchanging their *time* for a measly *paycheck.* As you know, time is the most *depreciating commodity* in existence. You can always get back the *$100* you lost betting against the Miami Heat. But you can never get back *100 hours of your life.*

If I've said it once I've said it a million times: True *success* begins with knowing what you want and doing what you love to do. There is no such thing as *work* when you are doing what you love. In fact, people who love what they do often have to *force themselves* to take a break.

I remember once hearing Robert Kiyosaki and his wife Kim talking about the time they took a vacation to *sit back, relax, and do nothing.* They were miserable! Not because they didn't enjoy each other. But more so, because they get so much enjoyment out of *work* that *to do nothing* was laborious.

I remember once being told by a successful businessman that when you are doing what you love to do, *the money will come.* He told me not to worry about the money. It will take care of itself. Most people suffer greatly in life because they never took the time to figure out what they're most *passionate* about. These people begrudgingly exchange their time for money. If you have never heard this before, make sure you pay attention to it now. *No matter how much money you have, you are unsuccessful without happiness.*

People who work jobs they don't like are *slaves.* Of course, that is not to say you are a *slave* just because you work for someone. What makes you a slave is when you *trade your freedom* for a *paycheck*. True *freedom* comes from doing what you are meant to do. Having a job might help you pay the bills and send your kids through college. But it will not help you to become *great* as I describe in this book.

The main reason we wrote this book is to give its readers the key to *greatness*. Greatness cannot be achieved through the accumulation of money. Although Len Bias was a noted basketball star, Len never achieved *greatness*. Greatness also cannot be achieved by becoming world famous. Count Gottfried von Bismarck was as well connected as any person you could think of; but because Bismarck lacked this *key*, he failed to become *great*.

Greatness can only be attained by understanding the scripture *John 10:14.* "Jesus answered them, Is it not written in your law, I said, *Ye are gods?*" People who lack this understanding will probably believe it is blasphemous to suggest that a man can become *a god.* At no time in Jesus's life did he say he was here to do the will of himself. What made Jesus *a god* was that he understood the *key to greatness is obedience (Luke 22:42).*

Any man or woman can become *great.* The key is to learn how to submit your will to the will of the *Father.* Then, when you speak, it will be the *Father* speaking through you. When you achieve, it will be the *Father* achieving through you. Man will always come up short in his own understanding. But if he will only learn

how to *listen* to the *still small voice* of God within him, he will undoubtedly become *great.*

The main problem with most Americans is that they rely too heavily on what they learned in school. School does not *educate* students on how to become *great.* Instead, it *trains* students to find a job and work for a boss until they retire.

No matter what college you graduated from, your school did not *train you* on how to find your *purpose* in life and become financially independent. Schools should get a failing grade for only teaching you how to work for the rich. And unfortunately, many Americans paid good money for this *training.*

Schools should teach students that when they graduate from college and get a job working

for the rich, they are modern day *sharecroppers.*
Whether you know it or not, IBM, Apple, Intel,
Xerox, Microsoft and many other companies are
nothing more than *modern day plantations.*
Now, I'm not saying these are not good
companies to work for. But at the end of the
day, the people who work for them are working
for something they'll never *own.* Their *job!*

Even if you become a top executive at one
of these firms, you cannot *pass your job down to
your kids* when you retire. One of the key
differences between a rich person's education
and everybody else's is that rich people
understand what *property* is.

If you bought this book you own a *copy* of
it. But because James and I wrote it, we own
the *intellectual property* associated with it. By

intellectual property I mean that James and I own the *copyrights* to this work. Therefore, we will get paid every time a *copy* of it is sold.

To the average person educated in Amerikkka, their principle goal in life is *job security*. But to the rich who know the game, their principle goal in life is *property ownership*. Apple represents a *job* to the employees of Apple. But it also represents *property* to those who *own the rights* and licensing associated with the company.

Until you understand the importance of *property*, you will continue to be a *screw* in someone else's *machine*. Unlike most Americans, James and I are *self-educated!* That's why we understand things that most people with a Master's degree or Ph.D. do not.

People who intend to climb the *ladder of success* must also climb the *ladder of knowledge.* You can't just rely on the bogus information you received in school. School will have you thinking that your house is an asset. But James and I know better. A house is not an asset until you are getting paid every month as a result of owning it. Something is not an asset until it brings you *income* from month to month.

Because of the way we were educated in school, most of us only know how to beg for what we want. For instance, many Americans want the minimum wage to be increased. I disagree with this notion. The main reason I refer to getting to the *next level* in life as climbing the *ladder* of success is because the path to success is a *ladder.* Not a *bed!*

People who want the minimum wage to be increased only want to *lie down and be successful.* They don't want to get off their lazy asses and *climb the ladder of success.* Unfortunately, these kinds of people represent the *swine* of the earth. James and I are not writing this to *cast our pearls before swine;* instead we are trying to *shed some light* on anyone wishing to be enlightened.

It is preposterous to count on a slave master to *educate* you. In the eyes of your slave master, your best *position* is working to maintain *his property.* No one governed by a *spirit of competitiveness* wants to create *rivals.* But those who are governed by a *spirit of creativity* see *rivalries* as offering more *opportunities.*

By analyzing the world in this way, it should be clear who the true *children of God* are and *who are not.* Books like this are meant to educate *sharecroppers* who have been *trained and deceived with education.* There are plenty of works in circulation that will give you a better summary about the way the world works. I suggest you become a *student* of them.

The main point to remember about money is that *rich people learn about money at home.* Everybody else is subject to whatever they were trained to do in school.

Since 1904, the rich have *controlled* what we learn in school. Why would anyone with a *competitive spirit* teach you how to *play the same game* he plays? And the way the tax laws are set up in this country, it proves without a shadow of a doubt that *10 percent* of the population lives off the labor and ignorance of the remaining *90 percent.*

In the *new slavery*, the average white professional is more of a *slave* than his black counterpart. The reason is simple. *The more wages you earn, the more taxes "Pimping Sam" takes.* I don't think most whites in this country realize this. The only thing that helps to offset this fact is the *privilege* that comes with being *white* in Amerikkka.

What's also interesting is that *white tax dollars* also take good care of those poor black folks *living in the hood.* Who's picking the cotton now? White privilege in Amerikkka only *blinds white people* to the fact that they are Amerikkka's principle slave. *Whites have never been in the "Establishment."* They only *identitfy* with it!!! And as long as they *collectively* remain the *gatekeepers* of Massa's fortress, they can continue to enjoy certain *privileges.*

Remember, *anarchy* is the number one fear of those in power. To keep what happened in Egypt from happening in America, those in power maintain the façade of *privilege* for some, *underprivilege* for others. On the world stage, the only people who have real power are those who *print the money.* Everybody else is just a *white or black pawn* on the chessboard. And like all *pieces* on the chessboard, *pawns never move themselves.*

Like I said in chapter 10, most Amerikkkas are *machines.* And machines are not *intelligent.* A machine may be intelligently *programmed.* But it has no *intelligence* of its own. This is the dilemma that all *intelligent* people living in America face. It is the dilemma of trying to get a bunch of machines to *think.*

Machines buy homes because they are *programmed* to believe the value of houses always go up in Amerikkka. Machines buy stock because they are *programmed* to believe that playing the stock market is a good investment strategy. Machines invest in mutual funds because they are *programmed* to think these are good investments. Nobody bothers to warn these automations that they are being *taken.* For instance, *a mutual fund buyer puts up 100 percent of the money, takes 100 percent of the risk, and then pays the mutual fund manager 80 percent of the profits; if there are any.* Even if I were a slave to white people, I don't love white people that much.

Machines never realize the only reason *stockbrokers* are called *brokers* is because they are often *broker* than the people who use their services. I'm sorry to say but machines are stupid. In fact, many of them are currently paying a *mortgage* on a home that is valued at *less* than the property is worth. Why, because they *trusted* their licensed real estate broker.

Machines owe their *programming* to the school system they graduated from. Amerikkka is facing judgment because she doesn't educate her citizens to think intelligently. People who have little knowledge about the way the world works are the most susceptible to being *taken*.

And when these same machines come across an *intelligent thinking human being,* they often don't know what to make of them. Machines don't realize the only reason they believe *saving money* is a sound idea is because they don't understand the difference between *money* and *currency.* The real reason *paper money* is called *currency* is because it is supposed to *flow* like a river. Whenever *water* runs downstream, it creates a *current.* Hence, the nature of money is to *keep it moving.*

Burying your currency in the ground is the same as putting your money in a savings account. The reason this is a bad idea is because *your money is no longer backed by the gold standard.* If it were, it wouldn't need to *move* as often as it does to stay valuable.

Not many people realize how bad off Amerikkka is financially. The truth is, it takes up to *50 million dollars an hour* of printed money to keep this economy going. The only reason most Americans are not standing in bread lines right now is because America keeps borrowing currency from the Federal Reserve Bank. And every time money is *printed,* the *value* of it decreases.

Why would anyone store their precious water supply in a boiling hot pot? That's exactly what is happening to the value of our money every time they rev-up the printing presses. Constantly pouring more water into a boiling hot pot will not change the fact that eventually, *there will be no more water left.* That is why saving currency is an *outdated* activity. To get in the real game you've got to get your currency *flowing*.

Because of America's deficit, this country is becoming a *third world nation*. And in any third world nation there are only *two classes* of people; *the rich and the poor*. A recent study showed that among the *new homeless* in this country, many are *employed* individuals. Never before in the history of the U.S. has someone with a full-time job been *homeless*.

Who would have thought the day would come in Amerikkka where not even being gainfully employed could keep you from being homeless? In fact, a great many Americans are anywhere from *$30,000 to $50,000 in debt and unemployed*. This is the *reality* in this country. And to make matters worse, "Made In China" is the predominant *sticker* on most products being

sold in America.

There are many white Americans

considering moving out of their expensive homes

and into a R.V. (recreational vehicle). Among the

many concerns related to this lifestyle change is

the increasing *cost of gas.* The main issue with

the rising cost of gas is that recreational vehicles

never get good gas mileage. We're talking eight

miles to the gallon. The other major expense

related to an R.V. is maintenance.

And while living in these vehicles are less

expensive than living in a home, another major

concern with this lifestyle is safety. You are in a

much more vulnerable position, when you have

all of your valuables concentrated in a

nonstationary vehicle. Especially, when you're a female.

About seven percent of the homeless in Amerikkka live in rural areas. Even before the recession, about 3.5 million Illinoisans were struggling in poverty. Another study shows us that approximately 1.5 million rural homes are classified as *substandard*. For many of these homeowners, such substandard conditions started out with their lights, water, or heat getting shut off.   And before you know it, the whole snowball effect worked itself out.

I write these words not to study poverty nor the causes of it. *You cannot attract wealth by studying its opposite.* But I write this to show you that in Amerikkka, *wealth is quickly being transferred from one hand to another.*

People who don't understand the game are being left behind. And a lot of these people are *white*. The world is governed by *the golden rule*. In other words, "He who has the *gold*, rules."

As much as your teachers may have meant well, *they were not in control of the information* you received in school. Many teachers stressed the importance of getting a *good job* so you can retire on *Social Security*. The problem with Social Security is that it relies solely on the number of future employees paying into it. This is just *too risky* to count on. With so many jobs being *outsourced*, it's a wonder whether there will be any jobs left for Americans in the next 10 to 15 years.

With all the stories of doom and gloom going on, the hardest thing you will need to do is to keep your attention focused on success. Not to mention the importance of understanding "The Science of Greatness."

Many financial analysts these days suggest people *get out of debt* and *save their money.* This advice couldn't be more horrid. For instance, if you wanted to buy an investment property that costs $100,000; how long would it take you to *save* $100,000? And while you're doing your calculations, try to factor in your largest *expense* --taxes!

Most of the machines in this country who boast about their huge incomes never boast about *how much they pay in taxes.* If you added up all the income taxes you pay in a single year, it would equal up to about *four and a half months worth of free labor.* Imagine starting your new job on January 1st and not receiving a paycheck until some time after May 15th. The only reason people do not realize how much of a slave they are is because "Uncle Sam" takes almost half of their income *a little bit at a time.*

So again I ask you; how long would it take you to save $100,000? Whenever people like Robert Kiyosaki invests in a real estate property, he doesn't use his own money. He doesn't work a job tirelessly for 20 or more years to put the 100 grand together. Instead, he understands that *rich people use debt to get rich.*

If Robert came up with any money at all, it might be *10 percent* of the amount he borrows. But the remaining *90 percent* comes from the bank. This magic trick of taking $10,000 and turning it into $100,000 is called *leverage.* And like all magic tricks, leverage doesn't take 20 or more years to carry out. This same *trick* also works for *millions* or even *billions* of dollars.

Using this same trick, it might only take Robert *two weeks* to turn $100,000 into $1,000,000. But to do this you've got to get out of your mind the notion that *debt is bad.* As I lamented in another chapter, *debt is only bad when the borrower has to pay the money back.*

Buying a house and working hard to pay the mortgage with your own blood, sweat, and tears is *bad debt.* According to the rich, it's *bad* because *you* are required to pay it back. On the other hand, if you buy a house, accrue a mortgage, and then place a worthy *tenant* in your home, you will have created *good debt.* Overall, the problem that most *honest* people

have with this concept is that it seems to be
unethical.

But this is precisely how the rich get
richer. They create debt to purchase assets that
provide a *service* for someone else. In exchange
for this much needed *service,* the patronizers of
this *service* pay the rich a handsome ransom.

And here lies the *hidden secret* to riches.
In addition to asking the Father for the rich and
prosperous life you have imagined, you must
also pinpoint what *service* you will render to the
world in exchange for it. This is the *secret* to
acquiring what you ask of the Father.

Another point to remember about debt is
that it is worthless if you don't understand the
concept of *cash flow. Cash flow* represents two
of the most important words to the rich. Take

the cell phone for instance. The cell phone would have never been developed had not the rich been able to see how they could *gain income every month* for its use.

Once the rich understood that all cell phone users would have to pay them every month in the form of *a monthly cell phone bill,* the rich invested their money to develop the *service.* The key to remember about the cell phone industry is that as well as making a profit, these companies are also *providing a much needed service to the world.*

For most entrepreneurs, their main goal is product development. They create a product that sells and then *no more money comes into the business.* A cash flowing business on the other hand, generates income for its owners on a *month to month basis.* People who want to do well in business must first consider how efficient their *cash flowing system* will be.

Some examples of good cash flowing businesses are real estate, cell phone services, insurance, drug prescriptions, and on and so forth. If cell phone companies had only focused on *selling a product,* they would have missed a great opportunity to earn *residual income.* This aspect of cash flow also speaks to another important point about debt.

The key to debt is cash flow. Before you invest *other people's money,* you must first consider the potential for creating ongoing cash flow. Otherwise, borrowing money to buy things that don't bring you consistent income is *bad debt.*

And another point to consider about investing is that investing *is a plan* not a *gamble*. So many people think of investing as gambling. But true investors are only implementing a grand *plan* for building wealth. People who invest in the stock market are closer to gamblers because *they have no control* over the investment. They are like gamblers who find themselves *praying to the heavens above* when the basketball team they put their money on can't put a stop to LeBron James. This is not *investing*.

Control is what determines whether something is a good investment or a gamble. Before you invest your money you must first ask yourself how much control you will have over what happens to your money. This will help you to be more cautious about whether you are putting your money in harms way.

Another point about *investing being a plan* is that it is also designed to help you reach your lifetime goals. Whether it is money you want to accumulate or a dream home or car, *investing should be a tool* you use to achieve these goals.

You have to learn to think about your money as being something that is *dear* to you. If you owned a business you wouldn't send your *employees* into harms way. So why would you send your *money* into harms way? Things that are dear to you will have a greater propensity to hang around longer. You have to develop a better *relationship with money* if you intend for it to be a regular part of your life.

This point comes under the *law of abuse.*
This law states that *if you abuse what you have,*
someone else has the right to take it. As I said
before, the turmoil brewing in America is
because *wealth is being transferred from one*
hand to another. The main reason for this is
that those who were in power have *abused* that
power. And now, the universe is getting ready to
redistribute that power and wealth to someone
more *worthy* of it (Proverbs 13:22).

People who borrow money to invest must
also prove themselves *worthy* of the money they
borrow. To be worthy of borrowing money from
lenders, you will have to *patch up your credit*
rating. The same way you set a goal to save a
certain amount of money, you should also set
credit rating goals for yourself. You can start by
paying off old debts that have accumulated over

time. Make small consistent payments or see if you can *settle* with your creditors for a much smaller amount.

By paying off your old debts you are *clearing up your name* as far as being a worthy person to extend credit to. A lot of financial advisors these days suggest you *stay out of debt* or that you *cut up your credit cards.* They are insane! Using debt to build wealth is like the difference between walking to New York from Cleveland or flying.

As I have already proven, it will take you a lot longer to *save the money* you need than to just *borrow it. Credit* is your opportunity to put yourself in a much better position in life. So don't mess it up. It will take you a lot longer to become successful if you don't take advantage of the opportunity that comes with having *good credit.*

And another thing. You need to make *friends* with at least one banker. A banker is a good *ally* because when an investment opportunity comes along, you can make a *personal call* to your banker rather than an *unsolicited* one. If nothing else, your banker friend can advise you on why you were denied credit and how you could make your petition for credit more interesting to another banker.

You need to have friends in your life that can help you get to the next level. Associating with people who think on a smaller level will only make you think smaller. But why think smaller when you can think bigger? It is only natural that everything that lives desire to *expand* it's existence. *Wanting more than you have while thanking the Father in advance for it is the secret to success.*

Having a *spirit of thankfulness* is one of the magic ingredients to building wealth. But as you plan on being successful, you've got to look at your past financial mistakes in the right way. You must understand that in business as well as in life, *success can be a horrible teacher.*

There is very little you can *learn* when everything is going perfectly well. It's only when you *make mistakes* that you can learn what works and what doesn't work. To winners, there are no mistakes. In fact, *mistakes are resources.* And once you learn how to extract *wisdom* from your mistakes, you will become a powerhouse of knowledge.

That is why I urge people not to file for bankruptcy! No problem ever fixes itself. America is in trouble because *financially illiterate people* have been making all the major decisions. I'm not talking about our current President. *Barack inherited the mistakes of the morons of the past.*

Whenever you have a bunch of *stupid asses* running Fortune 500 companies you are going to have some problems. In Amerikkka, the American way seems to be *bailout all the bums who should be fired and replaced with competent leaders.* If proper actions had been taken, *confidence could be restored* in the American economy.

Only snotty nose children pretend to forget all the mistakes they made that put America in

the position that she's in. These *sociopaths*
often like to *scapegoat* other people so they can
walk away scott free from the problems *they*
created. And now America is on it's way out!

People who have made mistakes in the
past should face them! This is the only way to
turn your problems and mistakes into *resources.*
But if you *throw in the towel* and file for
bankruptcy, you are playing the *snotty nose kid*
game. Instead, I urge you to *play the adult game*
by accepting your past mistakes and fight your
way back to solvency. Setting this goal will
make a *hero* out of you. *You cannot become a*
hero until you first overcome insurmountable
obstacles.

There are too many negative implications
of *running from problems you created.* If you

were man enough to create them, you should be man enough to face them. Remember, you should always choose goals *for what they will make of you.* By choosing a *goal* to fight your way back to solvency, you will be adding more *power* to your current personality. There is no way you can come out of this struggle and not become a formidable force to be reckoned with.

And one last thought on credit. Remember I said that investing is a *plan*; well, the reason having a plan is so important is so you don't get *overextended.* One of the key skills of any good entrepreneur is knowing how to monitor and control *cash flow.* Often, it's not that people need to *make more money.* More money doesn't solve financial problems. Rather, they need to *reprioritize* the way they use money.

Money is a wonderful *servant* but is also a ruthless *master*. For that reason you don't want to fall into the trap of always needing to *run faster* to keep up with your responsibilities.

Not getting overextended financially means *planning aforehand how you will pay back what you borrow.* The principle mistake people make financially is assuming that credit is *free money.* Friends, *the bank is going to ask you for their money back.* Trust me. Of course, you could destroy your credit rating by pretending not to be concerned about this responsibility.

The only problem is, *no lender will be concerned about your need to borrow* if your name in the game is bad. What's the sense of developing friendships with bankers when you've already proven to be a *bad investment? You got to have good credit in this world!* And to have that credit, you've got to take care of it.

So, never bite off more than you can chew. You've got to look further down the line to see how you will be able to pay back whatever you borrow. If you can't *see* how you will pay the bank back, don't borrow it.

There is a scripture in the Bible that says: "The borrower is *servant* to the lender." But I might add that once a *servant* learns how to use debt properly, he too can also become a *lender.*

Being in a position to have *passive income* is a good achievement to add to your financial portfolio. Whenever you start a business, you are the *active principle* in the investment. But eventually, you will want to be in a position to *let someone else use some of your capital.* In this way, you will be the *passive* principle and the borrower will be the *active* principle in the investment.

The more passive income you have, the more *free time* you will have to look into other investments. This is the American dream. And by adding your ability to submit your will to the will of the Father, there's no way you can't become *great.*